A WILD
STATE OF HOCKEY

A WILD
STATE OF HOCKEY

The Minnesota Wild's
First Season
on the Ice

Thomas U. Tuttle

Beaver's Pond Press, Inc.

Edina, Minnesota

ISBN: 1-931646-27-9

Library of Congress Catalog Card Number: 2001097196

First Printing: November 2001
Printed in the United States of America

04 03 02 01 6 5 4 3 2 1

Cover and interior design by Mori Studio

Visit the Minnesota Wild at *www.Wild.com*

Address orders to:

Beaver's Pond Press, Inc.

5125 Danen's Drive
Edina, Minnesota 55439-1465
(952) 829-8818

to Corky Tuttle,
an avid sports fan
who has a great love of all sports,
and I for her.

CONTENTS

ACKNOWLEDGMENTS

This book was made possible by the contributions of a great number of people. I am grateful to the Minnesota Wild management for their openness and candor in assisting with this project while allowing editorial freedom. I am thankful also to the numerous players, coaches, trainers, scouts, fans, and arena personnel who took time to share their thoughts with me. I have tried to bring their words to life in this book.

The first year of a professional sports franchise is a busy as well as an exciting time for those involved in developing the organization. Special thanks to Bill Robertson, who has been down this road before and provided valuable counsel while taking time out of his incredibly busy schedule. His staff has also proven invaluable, with special thanks to Chris Kelleher, Brian Israel, Brad Smith, and Kathy Ross. Aaron Sickman made every effort to assist me, as did Jason Ball. "Billy Rob" and his people are the best, and it shows.

Jacques Lemaire showed his grace by answering my every inquiry with patience and honesty. Chief scout Tommy Thompson always took time to answer my phone calls. Through my communication with these men, I have learned what first-class people they are. Their love for the game of hockey shines through. I would also like to thank all the other coaches and scouts who spent time with me as I worked on this project.

Elizabeth Durfee provided valuable insights and meritorious suggestions that added to this book. Robert Tuttle extended his usual wisdom and good humor as I wrestled with the challenge of this undertaking. Doug Benson lent his steady hand and experienced vision. My heartfelt thanks to all three.

Jack Caravela of Mori Studio worked especially hard to bring high quality design work and creativity to this book. It is a privilege to work with you.

Special thanks to Heather Bernier and Pat Erickson of the Wild offices. I had great conversations with so many people that it is impossible to recognize all of them. I would like to thank all of those whose hidden contributions to this book effort helped make it a reality. To the entire Minnesota Wild organization, made up of high-quality individuals at every turn, thank you.

FOREWORD

by Glen Sonmor

I like to think that we brought some excitement to the Twin Cities with the success of the Minnesota North Stars, and gave our fans a few memories that they could savor after we were gone. The new Xcel Energy Center takes me back to the old Met Center, and a couple of our runs during the Stanley Cup Playoffs. In the 1980 playoffs, we beat Toronto and the Montreal Canadiens to reach the semi-finals. Goalie Giles Meloche was our Manny Fernandez, "standing on his ear" time after time in the Montreal series as we held off the four-time defending Stanley Cup champions. Doug Risebrough, the Wild GM, was playing for Montreal—and boy, he was a force on the ice, really a tough player.

In 1981, we went to the Cup finals against the New York Islanders. We had made a heck of a run, but the Islanders, with great players like Mike Bossy, Bryan Trottier, Butch Goring and Denis Potvin were a little too much for us. There's one good story out of that series, when they were leading us 3-0 and we were home for game four. During our pre-game meeting, I told our guys that it could not end tonight. It must not end tonight. We owed something to our fans and to ourselves. "Not Tonight" became our rallying point, and the guys played their hearts out. We beat them 4-2 in a game that I remember with a lot of pride.

I had Neal Broten in the line-up at the end of that 1981 season. He had come to the North Stars directly from the University of Minnesota, and contributed during our team's suprise run to the Stanley Cup finals. The next year, his first full year in professional hockey, he scored 38 goals to go along with 60 assists (for 98 points) and established the kind of player he was going to be in the NHL. Neal had as full a career as a guy could ever dream of. He was a tremendous player who won championships at a lot of different levels, and he had a lot of fun.

There were a lot of wonderful players that have come through Minnesota, and I've been blessed to be associated with many great people through the game of hockey. I'm grateful that I might have contributed to a few guys deepening their relationship with the game, men like Al MacAdam and Craig Hartsburg and Bobby Smith. Right there at the top with those guys is Herb Brooks, who I consider to be a hockey genius. My friend Lou Nanne has given so much to the sport of hockey in this state, at the amateur and professional level, that it's amazing.

This is a state that should have a major league hockey franchise, without question, because Minnesotans truly love their hockey. It's been great to see the emergence of the Minnesota Wild, and to be a small part of it. Tom Tuttle has brought back some of the highlights of the Wild's first season, the surprising successes, the strengths and philosophies of the new Wild organization and its people. This team will bring a lot of hockey joy back to Minnesota. In fact, it already has with a number of big wins during an exciting first year. Coach Lemaire has an aura of strength and a passion for the game, and he's a proven winner. What a great player he was as well. I know that someday not too long from now, with the leadership of Jacques Lemaire and Doug Risebrough, the fans of Minnesota will again experience the joy of playoff hockey—and of making a run for the Stanley Cup!

> —Glen Sonmor,
> Scout for the Minnesota Wild
> Former Head Coach, Minnesota North Stars

INTRODUCTION

by John Millea

The Zamboni parade through downtown St. Paul and the rally at Rice Park were history, albeit day-old history. The NHL had announced that it was returning to Minnesota, and my assignment the day after the big news was to interview a man named Robert Naegele, Jr. He was the owner of the franchise that would one day become the Wild, but for now he was the majority owner of a team that existed only on paper and in the imaginations of puck-starved Minnesotans.

I met Naegele on a late-June morning in 1997. The team had set up shop in a nondescript downtown St. Paul office building. A hand-lettered sign on the door to their headquarters said only, "Minnesota NHL hockey." They had no public-relations staff, no real front-office executives, just Naegele and what he called "a militia of volunteers."

The phones were already ringing. People wanted to know how to get their hands on tickets for the first season, which was more than three years away. The militia, mostly college-age kids who had been quickly hired, was doing its best to keep up.

Naegele found an office that contained only a desk, a phone and a couple chairs. As we talked about where he came from and where he wanted his hockey team to go, I began to notice some construction going on nearby. Naegele sat with his back to the window, and behind him I saw construction cranes going about their business on another new addition to downtown St. Paul.

How appropriate, I thought. The building of a hockey team.

In what seemed like the blink of an eye, those three-plus years passed and the new team was on the ice. The first workout at Parade Ice Garden was a mass of unknown faces. I looked for numbers on the players' helmets and then glanced at my roster. I learned how to spell and pronounce Sekeras and Laaksonen and Leschyshyn. Before long, thankfully, the faces and names became familiar.

On the ice and off, the Wild was built slowly, with great attention to detail. Xcel Energy Center may be the finest arena in the NHL, and Jacques Lemaire may be the best coach. Those are the kind of building blocks that bring immediate stability and respect to a franchise. But it goes deeper, into the foundation.

That day back in the summer of 1997, Naegele talked about "doing it right." He talked about not going for the quick fix, not spending wildly to achieve sudden but dangerously short-lived success. This is a slow process, he said, and we aren't going to get ahead of ourselves.

The proof was evident in the people he selected to run his new team. CEO Jac Sperling, president Tod Leiweke, communications guru Bill Robertson; they helped set the tone for an organization that wanted to do things right. Despite Minnesota's fervor for hockey, there were doomsayers who predicted the Wild would never find success in the Twin Cities' crowded pro sports market. But the team remained above the fray, politely asking skeptics to wait and see, to judge them on their product. Was there pressure on the front office, were there questions about its ability to make this thing fly? Certainly. And they responded magnificently.

The proof was evident on the ice. Other than general manager Doug Risebrough and his former Montreal Canadiens teammate, Lemaire, the Wild's inaugural roster was devoid of big names. Wes Walz? He'd spent the previous four seasons playing in Switzerland and Long Beach (an odd mix). Aaron Gavey? He played 28 games in the AHL one year before. Manny Fernandez? He was in goal for 50 IHL games two seasons earlier.

But almost miraculously, Risebrough and Lemaire put together a collection of no-name and never-was hockey players that gave us a remarkable ride through the first season. There was native son Darby Hendrickson scoring the Wild's first home-ice goal. There was the November night when Antti Laaksonen's hat trick—the only hat trick of the season for the Wild, as it turned out—beat Vancouver 4-2 at Xcel. There was the January overtime victory against the mighty Detroit Red Wings, the Wild's second victory over the Wings in eight days. There was Lemaire's public criticism of referee Brad Meier, which resulted in the coach (and general manager Doug Risebrough) being fined $5,000 by the NHL. And, of course, the still-hard-to-believe 6-0 throttling of the Dallas Stars in the erstwhile North Stars' return to Minnesota.

Personally, two memories stand out. The first is more politics than hockey: election night. The Wild were playing the Colorado Avalanche at the Pepsi Center in Denver. Having cast an absentee ballot before leaving on the road trip, I watched that Tuesday evening's hockey game with one eye on the ice and one eye on the press-box television that had been tuned to election results. Al Gore won Florida. No, wait, he didn't win Florida. George W. Bush is our next President.... No, wait, we're not sure. The issue was settled weeks later, of course, and the Wild ended up losing all five meetings with the eventual Stanley Cup champion Avalanche.

My favorite Wild moment, however, took place in Section 121 at Xcel. Instead of watching from the stratospheric press box, I took the night off and sat in Section 121 with my wife and children for a January game against the Wild's expansion cousins from Columbus. And what a game it was. Filip Kuba tied the score with 62 seconds left in regulation and Sean O'Donnell scored the winner with 67 seconds left in overtime. The place went pure nutso, and for the first time I could somehow FEEL the noise inside the Xcel Center, feel the emotion of the fans, feel their simple and utter joy.

Memories, wonderful memories. They will be hard to top, but it will happen. It will come someday, maybe someday soon, when the Wild make their first playoff appearance.

I can hardly wait to get back to Section 121.

—John Millea

MINNESOTA WILD ANTHEM

We were raised
With the stick
And a pair of blades
On the ice we cut our teeth
We took our knocks
In the penalty box
Our mother was the referee

This sport was here
Before we came
It will be here when we're gone
The game's in our blood and
Our blood's in the game
Lay us down under
a frozen pond

(CHORUS)

We will fight to the end
We will stand and defend
Our flag flying high and free
We were born the child
Of the strong and wild
In the state
the state of hockey

A big blue line runs around our state
A line that can't be crossed
The day they try to take this game
Is the day the gloves come off

(CHORUS)

MINNESOTA WILD
2000-2001 OPENING NIGHT ROSTER

NO	PLAYER	POS	HT	WT	SHOOTS	B'DATE	BIRTHPLACE	1999-00 TEAM
3	Ladislav Benysek	D	6-2	190	L	03/24/75	Olomouc, Czech. Rep.	Sparta Praha
4	Curtis Leschyshyn (A)	D	6-1	205	L	09/21/69	Thompson, Man.	Carolina
5	Brad Bombardir	D	6-1	205	L	05/05/72	Powell River, BC	New Jersey
6	Lubomir Sekeras	D	6-0	183	L	11/18/68	Trencin, Slovakia	Ocelari Trinec
10	Marian Gaborik	LW	6-1	183	L	02/14/82	Trencin, Slovakia	Dukla Trencin
12	Matt Johnson	LW	6-5	235	L	11/23/75	Welland, Ont.	Atlanta
14	Darby Hendrickson	C	6-1	195	L	08/28/72	Richfield, MN	Vancouver
16	Steve McKenna★	LW	6-8	255	L	08/21/73	Toronto, Ont.	Los Angeles
17	Filip Kuba	D	6-3	205	L	12/2976	Ostrava, Czech.	Florida
18	Cam Stewart	LW	5-11	196	R	09/18/71	Kitchener, Ont.	Florida
19	Jeff Nielsen	RW	6-0	200	R	09/20/71	Grand Rapids, MN	Anaheim
20	Maxim Sushinsky	RW	5-8	165	L	07/01/74	St. Petersburg, Russia	Avan. Omsk
22	Stacy Roest	C	5-9	185	R	03/15/74	Lethbridge, Alb.	Detroit
24	Antti Laaksonen	LW	6-0	180	L	10/03/73	Tammela, Finland	Boston
25	Sergei Krivokrasov	RW	5-11	185	L	05/15/74	Angarsk, C.I.S.	NSH/CGY
27	Sean O'Donnell (C)	D	6-3	220	L	10/13/71	Ottawa, Ont.	Los Angeles
33	Scott Pellerin (A)	LW	5-11	190	L	01/09/70	Shediac, NB	St. Louis
34	Jim Dowd	C	6-1	190	R	12/25/68	Brick, NJ	Edmonton
36	Sylvain Blouin	LW	6-2	207	L	05/21/74	Montreal, Que.	Worcester
37	Wes Walz	C	5-10	180	R	05/15/70	Calgary, Alb.	Lugano
42	Andy Sutton	D	6-6	245	L	03/10/75	Kingston, Ont.	San Jose
44	Aaron Gavey	C	6-2	200	L	02/22/74	Sudbury, Ont.	Dallas

NO	GOALTENDERS	POS	HT	WT	CATCH	B'DATE	BIRTHPLACE	1999-00 TEAM
29	Jamie McLennan	G	6-0	190	L	06/30/71	Edmonton, Alb.	St. Louis
35	Manny Fernandez	G	6-0	180	L	08/27/74	Etobicoke, Ont.	Dallas

★injured reserve

SKATING INTO HISTORY

The National Hockey League returned to the State of Minnesota in the form of the Minnesota Wild in the year 2000, following a seven-year absence. The North Stars, who left the state after the 1992-93 season to become the Dallas Stars, had come into existence in 1967 along with five other expansion franchises when the NHL doubled in size from six to twelve teams. The North Stars had appeared in two Stanley Cup championships, in 1981 and 1991, and produced many fine memories for local hockey fans. Their loss left a feeling of emptiness in the Twin Cities' hockey community.

There had been some question about whether the Minnesota Wild could occupy the same place in the hearts and minds of Minnesota's pro hockey fans. That question would be answered definitively on a brisk mid-December evening at the new ice arena in the land of 10,000 lakes.

The drive into St. Paul on the evening of December 17, 2000 was a time for reflection. Having just witnessed a tough, late-season Minnesota Vikings loss to the conference rival Green Bay Packers at the Metrodome, it was time now for devoted sports fans of the Twin Cities to focus energy on an important hockey game. Tonight the Minnesota Wild, a new NHL franchise, would host the Dallas Stars, the former Minnesota North Stars, in the 33rd game of the inaugural season.

It was hard to believe that it was just three short months ago that the Minnesota Wild's first training camp had begun in Minneapolis at the Parade Ice Garden. That September day was the first meeting of the 70 men who would be whittled down to comprise an NHL roster—the hopefuls, the wannabes and the experienced hockey professionals who would eventually become the Minnesota Wild. Of the various seminal signals of big time hockey's return to Minnesota, witnessing NHL players and prospects skating and checking and slapping pucks around for the first time was a breathtaking moment.

A man named Jacques Lemaire was sitting at a table above center ice, an elegant looking French-Canadian who would be judge and jury to the hopes of these chosen men. Most of the players were only slightly familiar with one another, in many cases had just met, and were now whacking the puck around like so many amateur players had done before at Parade. These get-to-know each other sessions consisted of four teams squaring off in a round-robin of simulated games. Amazingly, some of these men would be playing as a team in a pre-season hockey game only one week later.

While the hockey operation was gaining speed, the new arena, the Xcel Energy Center, was still coming together. Workers were pressing hard to put the finishing touches on what was expected to be a regal hockey environment. A 3-1 victory over the Mighty Ducks of Anaheim would christen the new arena in the first NHL hockey game, albeit pre-season, played by a Minnesota franchise since April 1993. Events were happening so quickly in every area of the new franchise's operations that one could only wonder if everything was going to come together in time.

The regular season's opening night at the Xcel Energy Center had come quickly, on October 11, against the Philadelphia Flyers, less than a month after the Wild had initially gathered for combat. The pageantry of opening night, which would feature the retirement of the fans' sweater #1, and numerous other celebrations in tribute to the many who made the night happen, as well as the action on the ice during a 3-3 tie with Philly, would whet our appetite for more.

The Wild had already played 32 games in a run that hinted at intriguing possibilities. They had shown themselves to be one of the faster-skating teams in the league with aggressive players who loved to forecheck. They played tough defense as a rule and rarely got outworked. Tonight, though, they would take on the defending Western Conference champions, the former NHL residents of the land of 10,000 sometimes-frozen lakes. In the devoted hockey fan's mind, this game was the big one. A lot of Minnesotans had probably circled the date on their calendar; December 17, 2000, knowing that if there was one game that they were going to see during the first season of the Minnesota Wild, the Dallas Stars game was it.

Some wags in the media had decided that a strong performance by the Vikings might bode well for the hockey team by somehow bringing momentum to the rink, and there had even been talk of a "double-header" of sorts in the Twin Cities sports community; a big NFL contest followed by high drama at the Xcel Energy Center. But one had to wonder if the Vikings loss to the Packers in a game with playoff implications might take some of the luster off of the evening's excitement.

This was an important hockey game for a Dallas team seeking to gain its 18th win of the season as well as for the Wild, who were looking for their tenth. Of course, there was so much more to it than just wins and losses. Returning to the Twin Cities seven years after the contentious departure of the North Stars, Dallas came into town playing reasonably well, but not the kind of hockey they were capable of playing, according to their coach, Ken Hitchcock. "We've been a little slow up to this point. We've got some injuries, and I feel like it's been a struggle to get the guys on the same page," Hitchcock said.

There should not have been any worries about the excitement level surrounding the game. There was a tremendous buzz around the rink as both teams warmed up for the contest. There was a playoff atmosphere throughout the arena as the Wild prepared to play their 17th consecutive sell-out at home, against the franchise that used to call Minnesota "home" before leaving the locals with feelings ranging from anger to sadness. The stage was set.

Talking to a St. Paul police officer outside the arena an hour before game time, I observed that he seemed to be stuck on the fact that the Vikings had dropped an important football game to the Packers. "Vikings needed to win," he grumbled, "Vikings needed to win." As we spoke near the Kellogg Street entrance, fans were pressing through the gates, energetic in their expectation of the battle they were about to witness. It soon became apparent that, at least on this evening, what had happened to the football Vikings over at the HHH Metrodome would be of little consequence for those fans who were psyched to watch this historic contest between the Wild and the Stars. The officer took notice of the growing swarm of Wild and North Star jerseys, and after a moment said, "Well…I guess we'll have to see what happens, but this should be a heck of a night for hockey," as he eyed the swelling mass moving before him. He paused and added, "I wonder if we can beat a team like Dallas?"

Departing from the man in blue, I encountered a young boy walking through the concourse with his father. I watched as he gazed in awe at the arena from the top of the lower level. Dressed in an old North Stars sweater, a couple of sizes too big, he looked spellbound by the hockey palace before him. Since he didn't appear to be old enough to remember the North Stars, I asked him about the sweater that he was wearing. "It's my brother's, and it's from the old days," he said somewhat defiantly. "I'm here to see the Wild beat Dallas."

So were about 19,000 others.

Defeating a quality team like the Dallas Stars would indeed be a major event for any new franchise, but for the Minnesota Wild there was, of course, the added historical significance. It had been seven years since the one-time owner of the Minnesota North Stars, Norm Green, drove Minnesota's NHL team down Interstate 35 and set up shop in Texas. Imagine if the Cowboys were ripped out of Dallas, or the Celtics taken from Boston; it just wouldn't be right. Minnesota hockey fans were crushed at the time, and many still carried scars from the sudden removal of their precious North Stars.

The new leader of the Wild franchise, chairman of the board Bob Naegele, Jr., spoke for many when he stated, "The loss of the Minnesota North Stars in 1993 was truly distressing for the hockey community in Minnesota. For myself personally, they were such a tradition and a part of our family life growing up that it felt like the loss of a relative."

Now, the Minnesota Wild were busy establishing a bond with the big league hockey fans of the Twin Cities and the state. "NHL hockey is reborn in our great state," Naegele had said before the opener a few months earlier. Indeed, a solid hockey franchise was clearly emerging, but this was still an extra special game for those with sour memories and sore feelings.

Norm Green did what he felt he had to do when he moved the team; perhaps it was a lack of suite revenue or a land deal that wasn't going to happen his way. The blows he took in the press regarding a harassment case couldn't have warmed his feelings toward Minnesota, and some speculate it was this particular controversy that really triggered his desire for a change of scenery. Despite the clear disdain with which Norm Green is held in this area, his previous ownership of the franchise that now resides in Dallas is, for all practical purposes, a moot point. He no longer owns the team, and he's had nothing to do with the recent success of the Dallas Stars, though he is certainly the man who moved the team.

No matter where you stood on the subject of the former North Stars, you had to know that this would be a special event in Minnesota hockey history. People were everywhere as the game neared, moving around the arena expectantly. The hum of an excited crowd, the type of buzz that only happens before a major sporting event, was in evidence. There were more standing-room tickets sold for this game than for any of the previous 16 Wild home games. Numerous political and big business honchos of the Twin Cities and the state were at this must-see hockey game, spread throughout the record-breaking crowd of 18,834, the largest crowd ever at the Xcel Energy Center.

On one of the four small balconies near the very top of the arena former Minnesota North Star Neal Broten was pulling off his old North Stars sweater to unveil a new Wild sweater underneath. The home town favorite was preparing to announce "LET'S PLAY HOCKEY!" to the crowd, and the fans were jubilant when those words were finally shouted. A look down upon the ice revealed former Governor Arne Carlson, instrumental in bringing NHL hockey back to the state, readying for the ceremonial puck drop. Time was taken to honor those involved in the construction of the long awaited new facility. The pre-game events were thoughtful and memorable, indeed. "I think we did it just about right," said Bob Naegele, Jr.

When the Wild took the ice for their pre-game skate, Minnesotans of all ages erupted in raucous cheers for their team, who represented a new tradition of professional hockey in Minnesota. The sound was near-deafening. "I really don't think the rest of our guys understood how much this meant for our fans until we went out for warm-ups," said Darby Hendrickson later. "The place was already going bonkers. I mean, they were waving towels and screaming and cheering. It was unbelievable."

The huge crowd was on its feet a mere 30 seconds after the opening face-off, when Mike Modano of the Stars, a former North Star, fired a wicked backhand from 25 feet at Wild netminder Manny Fernandez. It was the kind of save you have to make against a great team early in what was bound to be an intense hockey game, and Manny responded to the challenge. The fans roared their approval.

"That was a huge save, and Manny made a few others early," said Hendrickson. "I remember skating off the ice for a line change and hearing the noise of the crowd. It was an awesome sound and the whole team was pumped up. The atmosphere was electric, something like opening night but louder and with more of an edge."

Dallas applied steady pressure to open the contest, but the athletic play of Fernandez kept the Stars off the scoreboard. Then, at 9:12 of the first period, Wes Walz's backhand pass split the defense and Jeff Nielsen drilled a one-timer past Dallas goalie

Eddie Belfour to give the Wild a 1-0 lead. The native Minnesotan from Grand Rapids had put the new Minnesota franchise on top, and there was bedlam at the hockey palace in St. Paul.

A fan waved a sign amidst the madness that read, "You took our team and we went Wild!"

It was an exciting opening salvo that, while welcome, had arrived unexpectedly. Dallas had controlled the action for the first several minutes, yet here were the Wild with the 1-0 lead. Less than a minute later the crowd's happy insanity grew as Marian Gaborik netted his seventh goal of the season at precisely the 10-minute mark of the first period, the result of his deflecting a rocket launched by Jim Dowd from 35 feet away. Here was a dramatic Wild double-shot; the fans had not fully recovered from the exhilaration of the Nielsen score, when Gabby's goal was again pulling them up out of their seats, if they had sat down at all. It was 2-0 Wild, and the fastest two goals in the Wild's brief history appeared to stun the two-time defending Western Conference champions.

A powerful statement had been made. Dallas forward Brett Hull was skating small rings into the ice near the face-off circle and gazed for a moment up at the pulsating mob in the stands. While it was still relatively early in the game, something had changed. It wasn't just momentum, although "Big Mo" had certainly turned around from the opening minutes. It was like Minnesota had fired a couple of rounds into the body of a charging beast, wounding the animal and sapping its strength. Jamie Langenbrunner plowed into Jim Dowd in frustration, and Dowd deflected him with a glancing blow. The two engaged in a short-lived fight, and left the ice with fighting majors.

Dallas, the team that had applied such intense pressure early, was limited to a single good scoring opportunity for the remainder of the period and finished the 20 minutes with only four shots on goal. It was a stunning turn of events.

This was the Stars' first trip to the Xcel Energy Center and already it had been an unforgettable visit. Dallas badly needed the break after the first period, and nerves were on edge as the clock ticked down. Wild players said later that they could hear Dallas coach Ken Hitchcock yelling at his players on the bench to pick up the pace and start playing hockey. Wild fans could only wildly applaud their charges as they left the ice, the victors of round one.

When the Stars came back out after the break, they were skating hard once again and began swarming around Manny Fernandez with continuous offensive pressure. Manny, a member of the Dallas organization for six years, was ready for the onslaught, and later said, "I decided today was going to be a war (against his old team). It's not a time for friends or any of that; tonight was business and a chance to do something good for our team."

The battle was on, and the Stars blistered the Wild goalie with shots with a second period sequence that came with rapid fire. Everyone was firing for Dallas; center Joe Nieuwendyk rifled one blast, which was followed by Brenden Morrow and Mike Modano with solid scoring chances. There was a vicious flurry, with Duluth, Minnesota native Langenbrunner trying to stuff the puck past Fernandez, scuffling with the goalie and whacking at him with his stick, eventually falling on top of the battling netminder. Manny punched and pushed Langenbrunner out of the way, straightening himself in time to stop Jon Sim in front, and then Modano again on a pass from Ted Donato.

Manny Fernandez performed heroically during Dallas' high intensity stretch of offensive pressure, standing on his proverbial head to make save after save and exhibiting the gloved hand of a magician. Asked about his stellar goaltending after the game, he would repeat his mantra; "Like I say every night, it's not a one-guy deal. The defense played very well, the forwards came back, and that's exactly what we needed. That was part of our strategy, and something we emphasized before the game." Maybe so, but some of his saves during the second period were priceless, among the best of the year, and he was the man in front of the goal wearing the big pads.

The tide turned again as Matt Johnson, the big Wild winger, leveled Stars defenseman Brad Lukowich with a check. There followed one of the huge plays of the game just a few moments later. Darby Hendrickson was battling the Stars' Brett Hull for the puck to the side of the Dallas net, when Hull, under additional pressure from Johnson, threw the puck out front and onto the stick of a wide open Peter Bartos. Bartos rammed it home at 11:42 of the second, and then leaped in celebration into the arms of Lubomir Sekeras. Incredibly, the Minnesota Wild led the Dallas Stars 3-0.

The Wild bench was exuberant, sensing that they had withstood the champions' best shot and had somehow enlarged their lead, despite being outshot eight to two up to that point of the second period. Just two minutes later, at 13:41, the Wild took advantage of a wandering Eddie the Eagle, who had flown too far from his nest. Belfour, who had skated off to retrieve and clear a puck that was some distance away, was about to get burned when his clearing attempt ended up on the stick of a thieving Antti Laaksonen. Antti fired a pass to Darby Hendrickson, who drove it home.

It was not a smart move by what surely was a distracted and bewildered Belfour. The Eagle clearly was shaken, perhaps not just by the Wild's scoring barrage, but also by a slight blow to his pride at being outplayed by his former pupil, Fernandez. He now had even more to be miserable about. It was four-nothing, Wild. Belfour had been unhappy with the fact that he had given up a 3rd goal, and now, after the fourth, he was visibly upset, skating back and forth from one side of the rink to the other, pacing relentlessly. Back and forth, back and forth…

The crowd at the Xcel Energy Center, which had been watching the game with a growing sense of pure joy, was now beside itself. The promotional giveaway towels the Wild had produced for the game were being waved with a passion that hadn't been seen since the Twins Homer Hankies gained World Series fame. The blare of the horn after the Hendrickson goal was nearly drowned out by the crescendo of close to

The Wild whip Dallas. Mike Modano skates away following a Wild score.

19,000 voices screaming as one for the new heroes of Twin Cities hockey. That a Richfield, Minnesota kid would drive the dagger home with his fifth goal of the season, well, all the better.

There remained a third period to be played. The Stars possessed enough firepower that most in the oversized crowd were not entirely comfortable despite the 4–0 lead. It turned out that it was the Wild, in fact, who were not yet finished. A goal by Lubomir Sekeras made it 5-0 and at that point Dallas was a beaten hockey team ready to catch an airplane out of town. But at 15:43 of the third period, on a rebound of a Sean O'Donnell slapper, Hendrickson popped home his second goal of the game to finish the scoring outburst for the evening. The fans were nearing exhaustion from the onslaught of Wild goals and the vocal celebrations that followed. After all, how long can human beings be expected to sustain an unrelenting roar of excitement?

For some fans, the element of revenge on the departed Minnesota franchise was complete. It also seemed that this was more than just a thrilling victory. The joy of the win came as much from the quality and intensity of the Wild play as from the all-out mugging of the Dallas Stars. Something wonderful had enhanced the darker image of wholesale retribution. It was the fact that these guys on the Minnesota Wild, this bunch of scrappers who had been together for such a brief amount of time, had proven that they could really play the game of NHL hockey. It was an incredible performance on a very special night.

TWO

CREATING A FRANCHISE

Jac Sperling was in the right place at the right time, but he also created his opportunity. Bob Naegele, Jr. needed someone he could trust, someone who had the experience, to run the business. That man was Jac Sperling. The timing had to be right for the whole project. Good timing and know-how is what made the impossible come to life in the form of the Minnesota Wild.

For the NHL, returning to the Twin Cities was the right thing to do. Minnesota is a state that loves hockey and, despite the loss of the North Stars, always has and always will. The league wanted to work with Minnesota to make it happen, and having a savvy guy like Jac Sperling in the mix could only help to grease the wheels. Strong local businessman Naegele was able to bring in the best possible man for an emerging professional sports franchise—Sperling—who in turn brought in a strong manager to develop the hockey team, Doug Risebrough, who brought in the kind of coach who could flourish working with a "new team" dynamic, Jacques Lemaire. Just like a strong team, the organization had a great fit at every position.

Two hockey stalwarts who grace and strengthen the community, St. Paul Mayor Norm Coleman and business executive Robert Naegele, Jr., have their individual perspectives on the vision and the efforts that culminated in the return of major league hockey to Minnesota.

The Mayor

When I saw Norm Coleman in New York at Madison Square Garden prior to the Wild's January 14 game with the Rangers, and just after the Vikings debacle at Giants Stadium the same day, he looked pretty fresh. A lot of us were dragging from the effects of a long day, not to mention the train wreck of a football game we had just witnessed, and the Wild wouldn't play very well in a 4–2 loss to New York. But not Norm; he was bouncing around with his young son looking for Jac Sperling at the moment I caught him. Seemed like the native New Yorker had more fish to fry.

Coleman is still amazed by the success of the Wild project, given the constant challenges that came almost daily. "There were pitfalls and hurdles all along the way. Only providence kept it alive, because this thing was dead 1000 times, with all of the little problems and barriers involved. Jac Sperling knew how to deal with the league and how to overcome the challenges; it was Jac who really was unbelievable through this whole thing and was the magic man at critical times. Richard Burke (former owner of the Phoenix Coyotes) was the man who kept us at the table and hung in there. Pam Wheelock and Joe Reid, who both worked with me, they wouldn't quit. This was a very complicated deal that died a thousand deaths.★

"When we fell short in the Legislature in the spring of '97, we had nothing to show the NHL regarding an arena. Things looked very grim indeed." Listening to Coleman, one realizes that the whole thing came ever so close to being project "kaput," a good idea over and done with; heck, it *should* have been over, according to some political foes. Coleman continues, "This was the stuff of miracles, that every time a door slammed we found another door to walk through.

"We were told by the NHL that we needed to have a firm commitment; no abstract commitments, no promises, the league was *adamant* that we have a firm commitment by a government entity to build a new arena."

Coleman's opponent for Mayor at that time, Sandy Pappas, led the charge to kill any arena plan. Her thinking had to be that any arena plan would be unpopular, given the way a new stadium for the Minnesota Twins had been shot down at the capital. There was a lot of political hay to be made by opposing new-stadium plans; the old simplistic refrain of "no aid to the fat cat athletes and owners" had been a popular one in some political and civic quarters for quite awhile.

"I think the position she took was damaging to her in the end; it was a big mistake," said Coleman.

"The whole arena financing thing died at the state legislature on a Monday, and the next morning I called NHL Commissioner Bettman and said, 'Gary, you're going

---

★See pages 29-31 for a comprehensive list of staff and key supporters of the Minnesota Wild Project.

to read in the paper that this thing is dead, but don't believe it. Give us a week and I believe that we can stick to the original deadline and make it happen.'" That deadline was mere days later and time was running out. The Mayor needed to take quick and decisive action if his NHL hockey dream was to stay alive.

"I reconvened my people the next day and came up with a plan for the city to back the state part of the deal. That put us on the hook—*not only for the city piece* (of the financing)*, but for the state part as well!* Not a small number, mind you: we're talking about 65 million dollars. I then went to the Governor (Arne Carlson) with people from organized labor, the City Council and the Chamber of Commerce and asked for his support. The Governor said, 'I'll do everything I can next session to make sure the state comes through, I'll commit to that.' We had a special meeting with the city council on a Friday and came back the next Monday and passed a resolution in which the city guaranteed the state's commitment; so we were on the limb for another 65 million bucks. I think we got all this to the league on the day of the deadline, and by doing so we were still in the hunt."

By meeting the NHL's deadline, the Minnesotans were still on the short list for an expansion franchise, along with Atlanta, Nashville, Columbus, and Houston. But Houston had a conflict with an ownership group that was already committed to its NBA franchise, and that raised concerns with the league. Houston was eliminated by the NHL and the Minnesotans were in. The Minnesota group may have been the last party invited, but they were indeed going to the big dance. Franchise rights were awarded to Minnesota on June 25, 1997.

With the granting of franchise rights, the evolution of the Minnesota Wild had reached another growth stage. There still loomed another touch-and-go political battle in the coming year to get money from the state and relieve the city of its increased liability, but victory for now had been snatched from the jaws of one of "a thousand defeats," as Norm Coleman likes to say.

A look at the week Coleman devoted to getting Minnesota a professional hockey team showed mayoral "can-do" at its best. What an impressive run the Mayor put together in the face of likely elimination. He had managed to rally his varied troops, and stiffly refused to give in when NHL hockey could have been frozen out indefinitely. And, bottom line, he was able to get the city to step up and make the necessary financial commitment in the face of tremendous and ongoing negative spillover from the Minnesota Twins baseball stadium battle, as well as the Minnesota Vikings stadium fight. This was a large political gamble, taken by a man who saw the chance to improve his city and had the brass to take on the political risk.

"I was going to get killed if I left the city on the hook for $65 million. I was running for Governor at this point and you don't want that kind of baggage. We were getting squeezed from several directions at this time. Randy Kelly stood tall for us at the legislature and said that the city should not be penalized on this, that the state needs to come through. He fought real hard. And on the last day of the 1998 legislative session, the state did come through with its commitment."

Another meeting with Norm Coleman came just after his heady days of riding in the Presidential limousine, and a run for the U.S. Senate was in the offing. Don't count this hard worker out of *anything*. He truly was the catalyst for the Minnesota Wild and the hockey fans of not only St. Paul, but the entire state of Minnesota. Norm Coleman strikes me as the type of individual who is not happy, not fulfilled if he's not on the move trying to make something happen. He is a politician who moves like an athlete. The three or four staffers around his office on the day we talked seemed to share his energy, moving quickly from one scheduled meeting to the next as they kept up with him.

Coleman paused and looked at some pictures on his desk as he recalled the collective effort that finally made the Xcel Energy Center, one of the finest hockey palaces in the world, a reality. "Boy, without (St. Paul Companies Chairman) Doug Leatherdale and the business community..." his voice trailed off. "I've got to tell you, they (the business community) were kind of silent as far as appearing in the media is concerned, but they were big. The Capital City Partnership put up probably $350,000. It was the St. Paul Area Chamber of Commerce and Larry Dowell, and Dick Anfang of the Building Trades Council. The St. Paul Riverfront Corporation and city staff from Planning and Economic Development were great. You know, we had Jac Sperling on board, and we were putting together investment groups and filling out league franchise applications; we were doing a ton of stuff and we were doing it without public money."

In hindsight we can see that success came because citizens like Doug Leatherdale and the Capital City Partnership were standing behind the project, along with the building trades and the small business community and others. When Mortenson Construction helped with an application fee, they were hammered in the press, which perceived a possible quid pro quo arrangement with the team. In retrospect, they should be hailed as heroes for keeping the ball rolling. It took the creative genius of

Naegele and Sperling and Coleman, but without the civic support of the people of St. Paul, this deal would never have gotten done. There should be a picture of all these smaller role players in the arena bestowed with blue ribbons.

Has this whole thing exceeded Coleman's expectations? "Oh, absolutely. It's been phenomenal. You could only imagine how great it would be and it's better. It's better in terms of what it looks like, it's better in terms of the organization and its impact on the community." Coleman shifts from talking about the *deal* and continues to speak of the Wild organization. "That's where you get into the importance of having a Bob Naegele and a Jac Sperling, who brings in a Doug Risebrough, who brings in a Jacques Lemaire. They've built a quality organization with a real focus on the fan. You know, we had a dream and we got something started, but the most credit has to go to the entire Wild organization for what they've done to make it so special. Special for the fans, the people of St. Paul and Minneapolis, and the entire state."

Bob Naegele, Jr.

Bob Naegele, Jr. seemed especially appreciative of Norm Coleman's efforts to move the process forward and the Wild toward reality. "Of course, it couldn't have happened without Mayor Coleman," said Naegele. "Dan Bostrom, Mike Harris, Chris Coleman, and Randy Kelly were hugely helpful, and Governor (Arne) Carlson was absolutely key at the state level and in telling the people of St. Paul that he would do whatever was possible to make sure the bonding bill moved along. He stood tall in the face of adversity. But the mayor's up-front guaranteeing of the entire financial package—well, that gave financial substance and credibility to the project.

"It was the Mayor's dream, and he had a plan to bring his dream to fruition. He was going to bring together some leaders from the business community of St. Paul with the aim of returning NHL hockey to the state of Minnesota. He needed partners, folks who would be open to his vision." Coleman's dream was not necessarily a full-blown vision of the lovely Xcel Energy Center at that time; rather, it was an idea of somehow getting the National Hockey League to be willing to drop the puck in St. Paul, Minnesota!

Bob Naegele, Jr. is a man of substantial faith, and that is an important part of how he viewed his role in returning NHL hockey to the Twin Cities.

"We had a part to play in the Mayor's vision of returning hockey to the Twin Cities and the state. I'm a believer that God intervenes in the affairs of men, to challenge them and to enlarge them. And we had believers on board in addition to the

Mayor. Jac Sperling, Bob Naegele III. They saw how this could happen and I think we became determined to *make* it happen.

"It was 'Three' (a term of endearment used by those close to Bob Naegele III) who said to me back in 1996 that I should get in touch with the Mayor, that there were sparks involving a potential hockey franchise that might turn into a flame."

At that point Bob Naegele, Jr. was part of a group of individuals who had expressed support for the Mayor's project. It was later that Naegele would emerge as a financial lynchpin when the time came for someone who represented real money to step forward.

"It looked like perhaps we would have a shot at the Hartford Whalers, but that never materialized.

"On January 13, 1997 we made our presentation to the NHL in New York City at the league offices on Fifth Avenue. We were up on the 47th floor trying to do our best to make a strong impression, and we were pretty well loaded for bear. We had some key people from St. Paul with us—Doug Leatherdale and John Labosky, as well as Mayor Coleman. And we had the Governor of the state of Minnesota on board as well, Arne Carlson. Jac Sperling had orchestrated this trip to New York and we had quickly pulled together as a team. We did feel that the meeting went well, and in March of '97 we were informed that we had made the short list of cities in which the league was interested in placing a team.

"We were told that the NHL was going to come to St. Paul in April 1997 and take a closer look at us.

"The League wanted to us to be aware of the three things it was looking for, the three crucial elements that would tip the scales one way or the other: a strong market for hockey, a solid ownership group and a quality facility for hockey. And they wanted us to understand that we needed to score a grade of "A" in all three departments. They needed to see that we had a strong hockey market; we were at a bit of a disadvantage there. After all, the Minnesota North Stars had moved to Texas, so we naturally were forced to defend the loss of the Stars. That's called starting from a negative position. But I think we established that the hockey fans of Minnesota didn't leave hockey. Rather, hockey had left us, and we had a market that would welcome it back.

"Once we established our market capabilities, we presented our ownership group at the St. Paul Companies' offices, and there again, I think we scored high marks. Civic leaders like Vance Opperman and Stan Hubbard were there, reinforcing the idea that we were a solid group of community leaders with a vision. These were people who were willing to take a risk, a bold risk, to return hockey to our community and our state. We needed to convince the league officials that we truly believed that the return of the NHL was a worthwhile project, and that we were committed to its success. I believe we got the job done on that issue at that St. Paul meeting.

"So, it was now time to go visit the St. Paul Civic Center and show off the place where our team would play. If we had scored a couple of 'A's' in the other areas, we were in trouble here. The Shrine Circus was in town, and the smell of elephant dung wafted through the air as we toured the facility. We walked in out of a gray day into a very gray building with gray walls, and we were humbled. The surface of the floor was gray, too, as were the elephants." Naegele chuckled at the memory. "It was not the picture that the NHL wanted, and everyone who was there that day knew it. With that hockey arena, we could not and would not—ever—score high marks on the facilities requirement."

But a vital seed had been planted. Cinderella could go to the ball if she had a new gown; St. Paul could be a major league city with all the attendant benefits. So, rather then backing off or slowing down, those who were leading the charge for an NHL hockey franchise took advantage of the momentum and accelerated their efforts. There was a positive attitude among the leadership around town, and the Mayor was determined to capitalize on the support that was growing in the city. "This was when the Twins were failing at the legislature," said Naegele, "but we had some positive attitudes over at the Capitol and in St. Paul. I remember hearing a lot of 'attaboys' regarding our efforts for hockey, and that was a positive response, certainly, considering what was happening with the Twins.

"Nevertheless, when the Legislature closed in mid-May, the state was not going to do anything for us. 1997 was not a bonding year (the state considers bonding measures only in even-numbered years), so when the Legislature adjourned we were left to look to the city of St. Paul. I still think we could justifiably build a monument to the Mayor and some of the city council and civic heroes around St. Paul from that time. We were hoping for the state to come through, but we were really fortunate to have the city stand up. People like City Council members Dan Bostrom and Michael Harris really hung tough and were a large part of the reason we have hockey here today.

"First the city (and then the state) assured the financing of a new arena; whereupon we post-haste notified the NHL.

"When all the pieces came together, we were perceived as a very attractive city," said

Jac Sperling. Naegele continued, "We were then informed on June 17 that we were finalists for a franchise. The excitement level kept growing and on June 25th, slightly more than a week later, we were awarded an NHL hockey team for the city of St. Paul.

"How about this? On that weekend we had six thousand $100 deposits for season tickets. That was a remarkable number of people looking to get on board immediately, and it reflected the enthusiasm we had felt was out there.

"There have been so many wonderful moments in the past few years. I thought the regular season home opener against Philadelphia was very special, and went well from all standpoints. It was well planned and we kept the ceremonies to a reasonable length, I believe. The Dallas game was unbelievable, of course; I don't think I've ever seen players at any level in any sport match the emotion of the moment like the Minnesota Wild did on that December evening.

"But, you know, I'm a man who enjoys the process just about as much as the finished product." Naegele chuckles and pauses before continuing. "For myself and for a few others, it was like a 4½-year opening season. It truly felt like that. And there are a great many memories therein. I loved the naming of the team at Aldrich Arena, the introduction of the team sweater at the John Rose Oval where I skated with my grandchild. I gain tremendous joy and excitement from the games, but that's like the reward for our long and tough 'opening season,' which culminated in our making the Minnesota Wild a reality!"

To develop a perception of a strong hockey market in the Twin Cities was the challenge that Sperling and Coleman undertook. It is indeed hard to find a major league franchise situation more troubling for a league, or for a sports fan, than was the game of hockey leaving Minnesota. Major League Baseball in the state has thus far fought a tough battle for a new stadium, and the Minnesota Vikings are engaged in a new stadium initiative of their own. These are legislative skirmishes that have proven very difficult to win.

Norm Green, the owner of the old North Stars, had been selling a lot of tickets, but he apparently felt the need for increased revenue, while at the same time taking a beating at the hands of the media regarding an allegation of sexual harassment that would not go away. One reason Norm Green left was because he was unable to add suites to the old Met Center. He was going to be deprived of that revenue and he moved the team. There are those who believe that the harassment issue was as substantial, or more so, than the financial issues. There also are those who believe that Green had designs on, and plans for, the land around the Met Center, and that his inability to realize them also played a role in the North Stars' departure.

"I wasn't here, so I can't address that," Sperling said. "But he must have gone from the high of highs when he first arrived here, to the low of lows when he left." Jac merely noted his opinion that if Green had received his luxury suites, "the Wild would very probably not be here."

The Wild have created a fairly significant buzz following the success of the team's first year. Jac Sperling noted that, "To win the Stanley Cup, that would be a great 'high' for our franchise. That's the goal of this organization for the long term, to build a hockey club that is not just competitive, but is a playoff contender. You want to develop a stable of young players who play hard and understand the system. You have to develop players who can get you to that point, and that's what Doug Risebrough is in the process of doing."

Though they did not win at a playoff level in their first year, the franchise launch, including the play of the team, is regarded by many as a large success. But veterans of the league cast a warning,

Wild CEO Jac Sperling and Mayor Norm Coleman.

which the Wild view as a challenge: It's going to get tougher to please the natives who have been known to grow restless with expansion franchises that take too long to succeed. There's always that third-year reality check.

Jack Ferreira, former General Manager of the expansion Mighty Ducks of Anaheim, pointed out that a team's second and third years are inevitably accompanied by higher expectations. "First-year players on a new team are frequently out to prove that the teams that let them go were wrong. Subsequent years tend to reveal true character. There's more work to be done and perhaps a little less fun.

"The Wild seem to do it right. They have a blend of players with some skill who fit together well. Combine that with excellent coaching and a strong organization, as well as the fact that they play in a great facility, and there's a good feeling over there. But it does get tougher."

When you talk to Jac Sperling, you get a sense of the high regard in which he holds GM Doug Risebrough. It's in the way he refers to the man who he hand-picked to run the hockey side of the Wild business. It's also in the way he refers with trust to Risebrough's decision-making; there's a quality of belief that Jac projects regarding the work that Doug has done and is doing. When they talk to each other, it seems to be with the easy confidence of two men who are on a journey together to a destination neither can reach without the other. And Sperling has to have a certain trust in his GM; after all, he said, "We have people who know more about the business of hockey than I do. You have to hire good people and let them do their jobs."

It's a perspective that Sperling takes regarding the entirety of the business. "That goes for (Wild President) Tod Leiweke and (Chief Financial Officer) Martha Fuller and (President of the St. Paul Arena Company) Chris Hansen. You find people with talent and learn to stay out of the way and let them function."

Wild Vice President of Communications Bill Robertson recalled that it was early in the morning of the 1999 NHL draft when he and Jac Sperling were having an early breakfast, talking about of a variety of things related to the new franchise. Both men know a lot of people in the world of hockey and the draft, as always, was a great opportunity for networking. A good deal of their discussion centered on the steps being taken in the critical GM hiring phase of the continued evolution of the

Minnesota Wild. (Robertson has a knack for being around big moments in the early history of young sports franchises, having worked with the Minnesota Timberwolves and Mighty Ducks of Anaheim as fledgling operations before joining the Wild.)

Then who should suddenly appear but Doug Risebrough, who joined the Wild CEO and Vice-President for a little breakfast and some conversation. Whether a kind of lightening strike for Sperling, or a simple act of fate, it was certainly a stroke of good fortune. Sperling had been hearing about Risebrough, and here was a chance to devel-

"We Operate in Optimism"

"All of my life I've had people telling me, 'you can't do it,' so the critics didn't faze me," said Bob Naegele, Jr. during a tour of the new arena. "Critics are normally profoundly disappointed in people, and I don't operate in disappointment. We operate in optimism."

The former Dartmouth goaltender continued, "I knew that there was work that would need to be done. It was a case of, after landing the franchise, asking who could clean this big fish that we had caught?" He laughed. The message was now that big league hockey would be returning to the Twin Cities, who would be willing to get their hands dirty with the business of putting the organization together? What person would be willing to sweat out the challenges that any new professional sports franchise must face?

Naegele recalls that Jac Sperling was confident that he could further execute the mission. "He said something like, 'I can work with this thing,' and we knew his history of success," said Naegele. It is a record that includes assisting in the move of the Winnipeg Jets franchise to Phoenix and playing an instrumental role in bringing major league baseball to Denver in the form of the Colorado Rockies. Sperling was the right man to "clean the fish" precisely because he's the "complete angler"; a leader who has been on these missions before and has the business acumen to pull together this type of undertaking.

"Jac knows how the game is played and he's avoided the pitfalls that can hinder this kind of effort. He's put together a team where everyone plays an important role in the success of the franchise, and it was Jac who moved to get those good people into position," added Naegele.

op a feel for the man. Sperling is a man who places large trust in his instincts, and this was an exceptional opportunity to get a better read on one of the guys he was hearing good things about during his search for the right man to run the hockey side of the business.

Jac Sperling is a competitive man who brings a sense of humor to a lot of what he does. He looks for the same quality in the people who work for the Wild.

"One of the first things I noticed about Doug was his sense of humor," said Sperling about Risebrough. The ability to laugh is an important facet of a person for Jac Sperling; he injects humor into a lot of what goes on in his professional life. Sperling has a natural calm that belies the challenges taking place, and he uses humor to take the edge off. Jac likes to say that "People who have a sense of humor tend to keep things in perspective. I think they're easier to work with as well."

Sperling and Risebrough are a good fit.

Doug Risebrough loves to win. Underneath the good-natured, rather amusing fellow is "an intense, competitive, smart strategic guy," said Sperling. Risebrough wants to win and he has the will to win. Jac heard a lot of good things about Risebrough before he hired him, and found respect for Doug to be prevalent throughout the league. Hockey, like most professional sports, is dependent on relationships between management and players, as well as relationships with other managers. "There are 30 GM's doing deals with each other, and it's usually easier to get a deal done with someone you like than with someone who is a challenge personally. Also, I think Doug is sensitive to what the other side needs out of a transaction; if everything is one way you're not going to have a good professional relationship for too long. People who are easy to deal with are going to get more done, and I view Doug as professionally easy to deal with."

Sperling added, "He's a bright guy, he likes to read and he's a thinker. What I think he really has is an instinct for the situation, which is important in business. Part of that is developing a sense of empathy for the person who is on the other side. It's about trying to get things resolved in a positive manner, and I think he's good at it."

When Jac started interviewing GM candidates, there was a lot of speculation about whom he would hire to be the inaugural Wild hockey chief. As the process continued and weeks turned into months, the Twin Cities media natives grew restless. Why wasn't a decision forthcoming? What was making this fundamental decision take so long? There was talk that Sperling was unable to make a decision and was essentially procrastinating on his first important CEO decision. "The fact of the matter is that I couldn't make a decision because Glen Sather (the former head man of the Edmonton Oilers) wouldn't let me talk to Doug until after the arbitrations were over, which wasn't until the middle of August. After the arbitration cases were done, I was able to talk to him, and we had a deal by Labor Day. But I had a feeling, and Glen Sather had as much as told me this was going to be my guy, that this was the kind of person you want to have. I had met Doug previously and, though I didn't really know him, I had a strongly positive feeling about him that Glen reinforced.

"I talked to a half-dozen GM candidates, maybe more, before deciding on Doug. I started my process by calling most of the GMs in the league and introducing myself. I'd call them up and say 'Hi, I'm Jac Sperling, and I'm the CEO of the Minnesota Wild. I'm wondering what personal qualities and attributes I should be looking for in a General Manager. I'm asking because I haven't done this before, and I would value your counsel.' Almost everyone, to a 'T,' was very gracious with me, usually taking an hour or so of their time to talk on the phone. And in the process of doing that, I would find out not only what they thought were the right criteria and qualities, but I would frequently learn what they thought about a whole variety of people, without ever having to ask them for their opinions (about those people).

"It was a great experience for me to listen and learn from some great hockey minds, be it Glen Sather, New Jersey's Lou Lamoriello or Boston's Harry Sinden. One of the things about Doug was that it was very hard to find anyone with negative things to say about him. When you're doing background checks some interesting things can come up, but the great majority of comments regarding Doug Risebrough were positive. The stories I heard were that as a player he was a 'team' type of guy, and that characteristic carried over into his management style. That's the way he conducts himself."

Putting together a great scouting staff and an administrative staff was more important than going out and quickly finding a coach. Risebrough didn't believe that Jacques Lemaire would take the job. Why would a coach like Lemaire, a proven champion, come out of retirement and coach an expansion team? The most important factor was Risebrough. I asked Sperling why he thought Lemaire had come out. His simple answer: "Doug."

"There's a lot of things I can't do, but one thing I can do is pick winners, people who know how to win in every aspect of their lives. And they can make other people winners who are around them. That's how I characterize Doug and that's how I like to characterize this organization."

The Name and the Logo

A team must have a name, of course. Coming up with a name for this new NHL team was, according to Jac Sperling, an evolutionary process. How about "The Freeze"? That was one of the team names that didn't make the cut. (There may well be some very frustrated fans out there who are heartsick that the hometown lads are not called "The Freeze." As in "Go Freeze your..." Others, however, would say we do enough of that around the Twin Towns come hockey season.) "Fans didn't settle on one name at all, there were six that came under final consideration," said Sperling. From hundreds of names suggested by the fans, "Northern Lights" and "White Bears" were a couple of names that warranted serious thought before a judgment would be made. Also considered were "The Minnesota Blue Ox" and "Minnesota Voyageurs."

"Although we were deeply indebted to St. Paul, this had to be a Minnesota team. So we picked the name "Wild," knowing that we would join the NHL as the "Minnesota Wild." We unveiled the name and the big puck came out of the sky over at Aldrich Arena, a historical hockey site south of downtown Minneapolis. That was a special moment for many of us. The realization of the dream."

The Wild logo, the team's brand mark, would have to make contact with the fans and to celebrate all that is Minnesota and Minnesota hockey: wilderness, lakes and rivers, trees and sun, the North Star and the color green. (Which is sometimes construed to be a small tribute to the departed Minnesota North Stars.)

The SME Company of New York City does a lot of design work for sports teams and, along with Matt Majka, the VP of Marketing for the Wild, was largely responsible for helping to create an emblem for the team. Sperling stated that "we wanted to take the literal elements of the north and of Minnesota to help create an energetic abstract expression. We wanted to capture what Minnesota is all about, as well as what we wanted our hockey team to be about. Thus the wild-animal ferocity as well as the outdoor aspects of the logo."

The Wild work as a team even in their marketing processes. Sperling is very proud of the organization's propensity for teamwork. "It was a collaborative process involving a number of different people, which is the way we usually operate. As with everything we have done here, a number of people made significant contributions."

Overall, the Minnesota Wild rank second only to the Detroit Red Wings in merchandise sales. If you think about something as simple as a Red Wing on a wheel, and how that took off to become the number-one merchandise mark in hockey, it's rather amazing. The red-winged wheel, though not a literal expression of Detroit or its hockey team, is nonetheless an incredibly effective logo.

Detroit's logo became a successful marketing symbol by building upon a hockey tradition, which the Minnesota Wild do not have. Detroit speaks reverently of Gordie Howe and Steve Yzerman and Eddie Shore, whole generations of hockey players. Somehow, the Wild have built a strong franchise mark without the benefit of a long, glorious tradition. "Just like building a winning tradition without winning," said Jac. "That's the challenge."

The logo and the name of the new "Wild" franchise were on the puck dropped that day at historic Aldrich Arena, in front of a sell-out crowd amid flashing lights and a deluge of fireworks. The Wild name was unveiled to raucous applause. Sperling sees the name as having a number of different meanings. "It references a tenacious style of play, a freedom to live, work and play in our northern environments. And it reflects the state's wilderness heritage through an amalgam of Minnesota emblems."

Sperling tells an interesting story regarding the early media reception of the new team "mark," a marketing reference to a team's trademark. *Minneapolis Star Tribune* columnist Patrick Reusse had taken some playful jabs at the new moniker. "He was constantly ribbing us about our name, in kind of a good-natured way, calling us the "Skating W's." A couple of Thanksgivings ago he nominated me for a "Turkey of the Year" award. I didn't win, but came in second, which was even more insulting." Sperling laughed comfortably as he told the story.

Reusse, it seems, perceived the team's name was somehow a bit juvenile. "Patrick felt the name would probably inspire grade-school boys to want to come to the arena and had added something like, 'What would you expect from a guy who can't even spell his own name correctly?' referring to my first name."

"So, in more good-natured fun, I sent him a hat and a shirt made up to read, 'Minnesota Skating W's,' with the 'W' stylized. I enclosed a note in which I misspelled his name and said, 'Dear Patric, Thank you for the nomination, for which I am very honored….' The gist of it was that we knew he would be supportive and be there at key times. I also told him that if the "Skating W's" name caught on we would certainly consider changing the name on his recommendation." Then, when Reusse did a show on TV with Minnesota sports notables Sid Hartman, Mike Max, and Dark Star, he was wearing the shirt and hat. "You have to try to keep things in perspective and not take things personally. We had fun with that."

Patrick (with a "K") Reusse was seen at a number of hockey games during the Wild's inaugural season and he seemed to be enjoying himself, on one occasion talking to Minnesota hockey legend Herb Brooks in a relaxed manner up in the comfortable Wild press box. Perhaps they were chatting about the new plush digs in Xcel Energy Center or about Herb's assignment as the U.S. Olympic Team hockey coach. He sure looked like he was having fun. Though hockey may not be Reusse's favorite sport, he was a fair and valued observer of many "Wild" moments during the team's first season.

Sperling on "The Home"

Having a suitable place for a new hockey team to play had been a matter of concern for Jac Sperling before the NHL came to visit. It was a part of the complete package that the NHL wanted to see in place before granting a franchise.

"We had to convince the league that we had the market. And we did that. But there was quite a bit more to it. When the league showed up and walked through the Civic Center, they said, 'This is not going to be enough of a facility' " (Jac smiled as he said this, and you have to believe that even before the Civic Center tour, a guy as sharp as Jac Sperling knew the old arena was not going to pass muster.) "We had to scramble and work with the city and come up with a plan for a new building."

NHL Commissioner Gary Bettman had said in early April 1997 that a renovated City Center "would not be sufficient for a new franchise." In other words, the league was insisting that producing a new arena would be the only way to land a team.

It became a matter of building a facility that would meet the standard. The Minnesota Wild had a number of people involved in the process who were motivated by the notion of returning NHL hockey to Minnesota, including financial backers and political figures.

Sperling is quick to point out that the early Wild investors were people who could have made more money—probably a lot more—by investing in a safer venture with a higher rate of return, but who wanted to see hockey come back to the state. It can be argued that there was also a strong desire on the part of civic leaders in St. Paul to give something to the community that would be of substance. "We live in a world where everybody is at their computers, talking on their cell phones or stuck in traffic. We felt the Minnesota Wild could bring a sense of community. The Xcel Energy Center is a place where people can gather and share the experience of NHL hockey. That's what we're trying to offer.

"In that regard, those early decisions by our investors and the city leadership were made, really, for the community as a whole," Jac Sperling said.

Wild Movers and Shakers

Referenced throughout this book are several people who have devoted their time and efforts toward the realization of this Wild dream. The acknowledgement that follows is only a list of names and jobs...not nearly enough information to do proper tribute to the thousands of hours, challenges and triumphs faced by each and every one. The following comments are those of Minnesota Wild CEO Jac Sperling.

Wild CFO *Martha Fuller's* exceptional relationship with the City of St. Paul benefitted the process greatly. "She came from a strong background, (Director of Finance for St. Paul) and was supported by her husband, Tim, who is the City's Fire Chief, as well as a part-time amateur goalie."

Chris Hansen is the President of the St. Paul Arena Company and is responsible for making the operations of the RiverCentre Complex run smoothly. His many years of experience and honed instincts have contributed to the success of the Wild. "He's one of the very best in the business."

Ray Chandler was a "tireless and creative" project manager for the Xcel Energy Center. He had worked with Jac Sperling on the Coors Field project. "The grand job he did (with his top aide, Minnesota native *Mark Anger*) is a tribute to his wisdom and skill." Bob Naegele, Jr. adds, "To have a St. Paul kid (Anger) come back and make such a contribution is quite a story."

Pam Wheelock, now in Governor Ventura's Cabinet, played an instrumental role in negotiating the deal for the Wild with the City and the State Legislature. "She kept things alive when it looked like we were really in trouble." She worked in tandem with *Joe Reid* to make a Wild future possible.

Matt Majka, VP of Marketing, proved himself an invaluable contributor on all the business issues confronting the new enterprise.

Laura Day, Wild VP of Corporate Partnerships, was the key player when it came to selling out the Xcel Energy Center's Hockey Suites. "She was relentless about getting things done. No one imagined that we would sell out so quickly."

Steve Griggs, Vice President of Customer Sales and Service, was "The Ticket Scientist. He came from a background with the Toronto Maple Leafs and deserves kudos."

Bob Thompson, President of Fox SportsNet, and *Brian Whittemore,* GM of WCCO Radio, and *Stu Swartz,* the GM of KMSP, brought committment to the Wild well before knowing the financial benefits. "If they were operating purely on a commodity basis, we would not have been able to do these deals. They had confidence and trust in our people."

Former Xcel Energy CEO *Jim Howard* deserves recognition, as does current CEO *Wayne Brunetti,* for working to maintain a strong relationship, both corporate and in the community. "They've really been in our corner. We're proud to have the Xcel Energy name on our building."

Jim and Jon Campbell of Wells Fargo are "…invaluable partners who have been with us through thick and thin. Fans should know that the hockey jerseys of all the state's high schools lining the wall of the arena are made possible by Wells Fargo."

Paul Morrissey, owner of Capitol Beverage, "practically grew up in a hockey rink in Boston; it was a dream come true for him when he helped to return hockey to Minnesota, and we owe him our thanks. *Tom Marx* of Anhueser-Busch also provided much-appreciated support."

The Washington, DC law firm of *Hogan and Hartson* was "completely supportive of my efforts." Jac was a partner of the firm in the Denver office.

Lou Nanne was the one of the biggest supporters of the Wild from the start. "Lou told me, 'You guys are going to do it. You are going to make this happen for Minnesota.' He was our first and best advocate."

Richard Burke, former owner of the Phoenix Coyotes and a Minnesota native, "was the man who brought us all together."

The Members of the Naegele Sports Board:

John Thomas	*Rick Pepin*	*Bob Naegele, Jr.*
Bob Naegele III	*Jac Sperling*	

Minnesota Hockey Ventures Group, LP and Xcel Energy Center Project Senior Management

Bob Naegele, Jr.	Chairman	Naegele Sports, LLC, Minnesota Hockey Ventures Group, LP ("MHVG") and all subsidiaries
Jac Sperling	Chief Executive Officer	Naegele Sports, LLC, MHVG and all subsidiaries
Tod Leiweke	President and Chief Operating Officer	MHVG and Minnesota Wild Hockey Club, LP ("Wild"); COO of Saint Paul Arena Company ("SPAC")
Doug Risebrough	Executive V.P. and General Manager	Wild
Martha Fuller	Senior V.P. and Chief Financial Officer	MHVG, Wild and SPAC
Chris Hansen	President	SPAC
Laura Day	V.P. Corporate Partnerships	Wild
Steve Griggs	V.P. Customer Sales & Service	Wild
Matt Majka	V.P. Marketing	Wild
Mike Reeves	V.P. Human Resources & Operational Development	MHVG and Wild
Bill Robertson	V.P. Communications & Broadcasting	Wild
Bob Naegele, Jr. Bob Naegele III Rick Pepin Jac Sperling John Thomas	Board members	Naegele Sports, LLC, the general partner of MHVG

Ray Chandler	Project Director	Design and construction of Xcel Energy Center project
Mark Anger	Assistant Project Director	Design and construction of Xcel Energy Center project
Bill Morrissey	President	Morrissey Hospitality Corp.
Gary Cole	Vice President of Operations	Morrissey Hospitality Corp.
Keith Reardon	General Manager	Wildside Caterers
Steve Denny and Mark Pevan	V.P. and General Manager, respectively	Volume Services
Mort Mortenson, Tom Gunkel, John Wood, Steve Halverson, Ralph McCoy	Owner, President, VP, former VP, Project Director	MA Mortenson
Richard Copeland	Owner	Thor Construction
Wayne London	Project Manager	HOK Sport (Architects)
Helpful Parties		
Pam Wheelock	Chief negotiator for the City, former City Lease Rep.	Director of Finance for the State of Minnesota in Governor Ventura's cabinet
Joe Reid	Former City Lease Rep.	Former City Budget Director
Erich Mische	City Lease Rep.	Executive Director of River Centre Authority
Jay Benanav Jerry Blakey Dan Bostrom Chris Coleman Dino Guerin Michael Harris	City Council Members from 1996 to Present	City Council

Patrick Harris Kathy Lantry Bobbi Megard Gladys Morton		
Jim Reiter Janice Rettman Dave Thune	City Council Members from 1996 to Present	City Council
Rick Aguilar Richard Beeson Dan Bostrom Chris Coleman Don Del Fiacco Gary Fields Richard Ginsberg Michael Harris LeClair Lambert Rich O'Connor Joe O'Neill Robert Schwartzbauer Mark Shields Lois West Duffy Richard Zehring (Chair)	RiverCentre Authority Members from 1996 to Present	RiverCentre Authority
Sen. Randy Kelly & Rep. Alice Hausman	Legislative sponsors to bill authorizing new arena	Legislature
Arne Carlson	Former Governor	Governor of Minnesota
Dick Anfang	Executive Secretary	Building Trades Council
Larry Dowell	President	Saint Paul Area Chamber of Commerce
Doug Leatherdale & Al Schuman	Chair and former Chair of Capital City Partnership, respectively	Chairman of St. Paul Cos. and Ecolab, respectively

THREE

BUILDING A TEAM

"I think one of the biggest challenges that we have faced is to build a winning tradition knowing that it is likely we won't win immediately." Jac Sperling was speaking candidly as he enjoyed one of his fine Dominican cigars, (the short kind that he seems to favor), and recognized the irony of his words: to build a winning tradition without winning a majority of your games. "That's been part of the magic here," said a reflective Sperling.

The Minnesota Wild have indeed created a magical bond with the fans, and perhaps gained the trust of those more rabid hockey followers who have jumped on the bandwagon now in anticipation of the more consistent winning that is likely to follow. "I'm not sure how we are doing it, although the big wins help, and the huge victory over Dallas has to have had a very positive impact" said Sperling. "(Wild President) Tod Leiweke and his people have done a grand job of keeping the fans excited. It's a special thing the way that this hockey team has connected with its fans, and a rewarding part of our growth process."

When Doug Risebrough brought in his old teammate Jacques Lemaire to coach the team, the discerning hockey fan realized that a master of defensive hockey would be at the helm of the brand new club. Good news for a young team, to learn to play smart, defense-oriented hockey that would keep them in games as they became a stronger unit. This is a team that needs to be developed, nurtured, allowed to gain confidence. There would be opportunities to attack, lots of them, in every game, if the Wild men were willing to work hard enough.

The Wild have earned the respect of the NHL hockey-hungry fans of the Twin Cities by playing the type of hard-working, solid-checking fundamental hockey that the knowledgeable puck watchers of Minnesota appreciate. It didn't take long for Wild fans to realize that their team played hard every time they were out on the ice; win, lose or draw. They came to love the effort and grew to love the players (in short order). And the passion for the team grew with the passing of each on-ice battle. The Minnesota Wild come to play, at the Xcel Energy Center or on the road.

There are a number of people around the NHL who have been impressed by the way the Wild organization has been put together, along with the speed with which the team became competitive.

Vancouver Canuck President and GM Brian Burke has high regard for the Wild management team, as well as the team that has come together on the ice. Burke is a candid person, honest and sincere about the sport he loves. He is the kind of guy who, out of courtesy, returns phone calls the same day from media people he doesn't know well.

"They haven't made any mistakes getting out of the gate," said the man who heads the proud Canuck franchise. "They've put talented people at every position, and I have found over the years that the success of a franchise is invariably tied to the quality of the front office."

Burke spoke of Wild president Tod Leiweke as an example of the attitude toward teamwork that he believes permeates the Minnesota operation. "Tod is spoken of reverentially around here, from the days when he served in our organization (Leiweke was executive vice president of Orca Bay Sports and Entertainment, which oversaw the basketball Grizzlies as well as the Canucks, from 1995-98). He was regarded as a great strategic thinker who brought a lot to the table, both in style and substance. Those are the kind of guys they have; everybody strong at what they do.

"The Wild are a textbook example of how to handle an expansion franchise. They have a well-liked owner with vision and brains, superstars in every key position, from Jac Sperling all the way down through the hockey department. They also hired a St. Paul guy, Bill Robertson (Wild VP of Communications and Broadcasting) who was set for life out in Anaheim. That was a stroke of genius.

"There's nobody in the business better than Billy Rob."

Burke likes the way the Wild have integrated themselves into the community, which was no surprise to him given his knowledge of the Twin Cities and the people "driving the bus" of the Wild operation. He also thinks that linking the team to a sort of grass-roots hockey movement "was brilliant. They want to tangibly give back to the community and earn the loyalty that kind of commitment brings. They want to get their message out there and the whole thing has been a great success."

Lest it all sounded too good or too easy, however, Burke noted that the Wild would doubtless face some pitfalls as they marched forward.

"They came out of the chute full speed," said the Canuck executive (who enjoys the study of military history in what little free time he has). "They have a very sophisticated audience in the Twin Cities, a crowd that really knows hockey. They *had* to put together a team that would be fairly competitive from the start; you have a fan base that knows the game and wants to see good hockey.

"If a few years down the road they look back and say, 'well, we could have had Ilya Kovalchuk (number one draft choice overall in the 2001 entry draft), but we needed to win,' that might be a problem. Let's imagine Kovalchuk becomes a big star, then maybe in 10 years you wonder if it was so important to be in a hurry to be competitive. But, again, the market requires a team that can play."

Building the Team

The task of putting together a group of players and finding a coach who could turn them into "a team that can play" fell on the shoulders of Wild GM Doug Risebrough. To appreciate how he went about doing that, it's important to understand that Risebrough views the ability to play in the NHL as a privilege and not a right. A player has to respect the game, his teammates and his hockey organization if he is going to know true success. Part of this attitude has to be attributable to the system in which he was a player, along with Jacques Lemaire and Mario Tremblay, in Montreal. It was a kind of brotherhood when you joined *Les Habitants,* and Doug is a member in good standing of the powerhouse organization that was the Montreal Canadiens of the late 1970's.

Risebrough clearly remembers the feeling when Montreal won four consecutive Stanley Cups, from 1976 to 1979. He recalls the caliber of people he was working with when they were champions, and he wants to project as much of that competitive reality as possible to the Minnesota Wild. Though subject to the winds of change, great people and a great organization are a constant with winning hockey programs.

"I look for players who I know are going to enjoy the game *and who are respectful of the game"* said Risebrough. "It's hard work being a player in today's game, certainly more work than 20 years ago, more confusing, with a lot more distractions. There's more responsibility with the money these guys earn, and they generally weather everything better if they demonstrate that they really enjoy playing and have the proper respect for the game."

Risebrough's greatest success has to be the quality of players and personnel he was able to secure. He told the ownership, after being hired on September 2, 1999, that he was going to bring in a superior staff to build the highest quality hockey organization. The only thing was, with the inaugural training camp beginning in less then a year, who were those people going to be?

"I had people say to me, 'Why would you want to take on a situation like that?'" Doug recalls. "My response was, well, if that's the only obstacle, why would you *pass up* a job like that? And I told them (the Wild ownership group) that within a year, I would have a staff, in terms of scouting, that is second to none. I believe we've done that a lot quicker than even I expected."

Doug's relationships with people he had known in the game helped him greatly while putting together his staff. He knew Wild chief scouts Tommy Thompson and

Tod Leiweke, Doug Risebrough, Jacques Lemaire, Jac Sperling, Bob Naegele, Jr.

Guy Lapointe (a member of six Stanley Cup teams as a player, and a member of the Hockey Hall of Fame) personally and had worked with both in the past. "It was all about relationships," he said firmly. "People whom I had worked for or worked against would come forward to tell me about somebody, or suggest that a particular person could help me. Glen Sather was willing to let a guy like Tommy Thompson go because he thought it was a good career opportunity for him. There was a high level of recruitment, I believe, and that started the ball rolling."

The relationship between Doug and Jacques Lemaire is clearly one of sincere mutual respect. What is also interesting is the way Doug references Jacques, with what at times seems almost like gratitude that Lemaire would consider working for, and with, him. But Jacques Lemaire would not have come to the Wild were it not for the presence of Doug Risebrough.

"Jacques' interest in the job was clearly a big part of pulling things together," Risebrough said. "Assembling a coaching staff with the track record that they have, the winning tradition and also the patience to develop players, set a kind of framework that showed we were not (about being) an expansion team," he continued. "In fact, we never used the word 'expansion' all year. We used the word 'new' on occasions when we needed a word to describe what we were doing. This was not an expansion setting. We were a new team with a goal of winning in the NHL, with a long-term plan of continuing to win. I think our coaching staff brings us to another level, as far as what our expectations are."

It happened very quickly, it seemed to many Wild followers. All of a sudden, after big victories and hard-fought hockey games started to blend together, these guys were not perceived as an expansion team. If that was an early label in the public eye or in the media, it was being shed around the Xcel Energy Center. This was a squad putting it all on the line with a cast of young players and desire-driven veterans. These were professionals with pride who had set about the mission of earning respect as a *hockey team*, not as an *expansion team*.

Finding the coach

Much of the impetus for this first-year team's surprising level of success came from the coach. Finding and hiring that coach had been the culmination of a great deal of thought and discussion.

"I had been thinking about the type of coaches I liked since I left the coaching ranks," Risebrough said. "For a guy who didn't spend a lot of time in coaching, I have asked a lot of questions about coaches and about different styles of coaching. I asked questions for three years about the best coaches teams had, and I wasn't even hiring coaches then. The two names that came up automatically, all the time, were Jacques Lemaire and Pat Quinn."

Pat Quinn is a fiery individual, with a personality that is both intense and gung ho. As a player, he was one of the few guys in the league who would go after Bobby Orr, and then have the whole Boston team bearing down on him, usually with little support from his teammates. He had a little problem during the 2001 Stanley Cup playoffs when he physically tossed a photographer off an elevator, during a time when he was being asked a lot of questions regarding Tie Domi's cheap shot on Scott Niedermayer during the Stanley Cup Playoffs. Quinn is the real deal, as proven by his success in Toronto, and might have been a good coach for the Wild. But he would not have been Jacques Lemaire, whom Scott Taylor of the Winnipeg Free Press calls, "My coach of the year, hands down. What he did with those guys in 2000–2001 is utterly amazing! It was the best coaching job I've seen in my 26 years around the game as a working journalist."

The hockey brain trust: Risebrough and Lemaire.

At the end of February, 2000 Risebrough talked to his friend Rejean Houle, the General Manager of the Montreal Canadiens, to get his opinion on whether Jacques Lemaire might be interested in coaching hockey again. The answer he received did nothing to discourage the new Wild GM from continuing to think in terms of Jacques as a potential coach for the Wild. Houle and

Risebrough were friends who had played together in Montreal during the high times of the Habs, and Risebrough trusted and respected his former teammate.

"Reggie and I had a close enough relationship that I felt I could ask him his thoughts on Jacques, with whom we had played in Montreal," began Risebrough. "I asked him if he thought Jacques was interested in coaching again and Reggie, with his typical straightforward honesty, said yes, he thought he was. But he also told me that Jacques would not coach in Montreal again."

Jacques had stepped away from coaching the Canadiens after the 1984-1985 season, a year in which he had won 41 games (41-27-12) and taken the team into the second round of the playoffs. He didn't coach again until the 1993-1994 season with New Jersey, winning the Cup the following year. He departed from the Devils after the 1997-1998 campaign, a year in which the team won 48 games (48-23-11) and was defeated in the first round of the playoffs. The loss didn't sit well with Lemaire, and he has often said that he had done all he could with that squad.

When the New Jersey Devils hit empty in the '98 Cup playoffs, so too was Jacques Lemaire left hollow. He walked away from the game completely on his own terms. Clearly, this is a man who operates by his own motives and formulates his own challenges.

"Experience was an important factor for me, although most of the expansion teams had gone with guys with no experience when hiring coaches," said Risebrough. "I felt that experience was a bigger factor than most people may have considered with a new team. Here's a guy who knew the game, who had credibility in winning, who could relate well to the players. And a guy who could really teach, which is what we wanted to do here. So Jacques was the fit. I hoped he would want to coach again, but I didn't know. That's why I asked Reggie (Houle) if Jacques wanted to coach, and if Reggie had said 'no,' well, then I would have had to look elsewhere. He said to me 'I think he wants to, but you're going to have to ask him.'

"Again, I wasn't in a position to hire a coach and I wasn't even working for this organization, but I remember those things constantly coming up in answer to my questions. I would ask people 'Why do you feel strongly about him? Why do you like that guy? Why was he a good coach for you?' Each would explain how he saw different people, and ultimately I formulated this model of the kind of coach I would want, and the guy who filled the bill was Jacques."

With rumors circulating regarding whom Doug was considering for the coaching job, Risebrough knew that his pursuit of Lemaire would be a big story in Montreal. He was determined to keep a low profile and stay on course to find the coach he wanted, after the draft if need be, and was not going to be rushed.

"I needed the best coach, and if the best coach was going to be hired after the draft, then so be it." said Risebrough. "When I went to see Jacques down in Florida, I was really inspired by our initial conversation and I developed a feeling right away. We didn't talk about the Wild setting in particular, but rather about hockey in general. I came to the conclusion that he wanted to coach again by the way that he talked. We went fishing, and I felt good about the way it was going.

"You know, it was good to be talking with Jacques again."

The way Lemaire was responding positively to the coaching inquiry was making Risebrough feel better, and the plot was thickening in the hot Florida sun. "We had a couple more conversations, and they were progressing well. Between the first of April to the end of May we had three discussions and I felt that real progress was being made."

One of the meetings was in St. Paul, and as is the Risebrough custom of insuring privacy, he booked Jacques under an assumed name at the Saint Paul Hotel; a *female* name. "It had to be tough for him when he arrived at the front desk," laughed Risebrough.

After one of their meetings, things were looking very good to Risebrough. It appeared to the Wild GM that he may have landed his man. As they were parting after a final meeting, Lemaire turned to Risebrough and asked him for a sweater. Jacques wanted to see what the Minnesota Wild sweater was going to look like, and he wanted one. "I originally thought that he just wanted to see the sweater," remembered Risebrough. "Then I realized he wanted to really look at the sweater, he wanted to see the colors and the crest. I knew that he wanted to see for himself how inspiring this jersey was going to be.

"There was a problem, though. We had sold so much merchandise, we didn't have a sweater! So I dropped him off at the airport and told him I'd send him a sweater immediately. When I got back to the office, nobody could come up with a sweater. I wasn't going to send him a replica sweater, it had to be an authentic, Minnesota Wild sweater that the players were going to play in. We finally found one in New York and had it express-mailed to him the next day."

After talking it over with his family and giving it some final thought, Lemaire agreed to a deal that was finalized and announced to the public on June 19, 2000. The draft was only a few days away, and after the news conference in St. Paul, it was off to Calgary for the expansion and entry draft processes. The former Montreal Canadien teammates and Stanley Cup champions were together once again.

Jacques Lemaire

Jacques Lemaire is a strong, silent man, with a natural charm that belies his reputation for having icewater in his veins. Not physically imposing at 5' 10" and a still-trim 180 pounds, his intense, albeit calm, demeanor nevertheless gives him a definite presence. A feisty forward from 1967 to 1979 for the Montreal Canadiens—"Les Habitants"—the greatest organization in the history of his sport, he collected eight Stanley Cup championships as a player (though not eight rings; the first few championships preceded the awarding of that now-familiar symbol) and two more while working in the Hab's front office.

Following the 1993–1994 season, his first as coach of the New Jersey Devils, Lemaire was awarded the Jack Adams Trophy as the NHL's top coach, and in 1994–1995 he led the Devils to their first-ever Stanley Cup championship.

Lemaire has a strong personality, but an honest and warm nature as well. He is quick with a smile, and the smile is genuine. Visitors to his office at the Xcel Energy Center navigate a labyrinth of stairways and corridors before arriving at his office. This is a hockey man's place of business: a cubbyhole decorated, aside from a few pieces of family memorabilia, with the accoutrements of hockey just about everywhere—on tables, in folders, on charts and blackboards.

Lemaire has a system for playing his brand of hockey, and it was his intention to get the guys on this new team to understand what he needed from them. His own experience, as a player with the Canadiens and as a coach with the Canadiens and the Devils, was that there can be only one leader. For the Minnesota Wild, that would be Jacques Lemaire.

"I was interested in getting a good start as far as control," Lemaire said, his voice tapering off on the word 'control.' He continued, "I mean that when there is good control in the organization you are able to position yourself to start moving in the right direction to have success. Some of that involves respect, and getting the guys to believe in what we are trying to do. This is control in a very broad sense; we're talking about a lot of things with the hockey team when we speak of control."

Of course, this was especially true with a new team. Lemaire knew that his new

Wild bunch had no reference points whatsoever as a unit, no history, and only a vague sense of the future. He became the focal point for his young squad. "You have to have a sense of discipline, discipline with the players and with the staff, and a sense of what we are trying to accomplish," he said firmly, looking again at the names on the wall. "My job is to bring the hockey part, to have a bunch of guys who will care for the organization, who will want to play here for me. I want them to have fun and be able to express themselves as much as they can on the ice."

Lemaire paused for a moment, and added: "I had to be the leader."

And the leader he is. Players on the Wild recognize the formidable hockey history behind their coach. "He's a guy who has been there and done a lot of things on the ice that we are aware of as players," says Darby Hendrickson. "The facts of his playing and coaching career have to help us to listen when he is on the ice teaching." Scott Pellerin spoke just as respectfully a few days after he was traded from the Wild. "Bar none, Jacques Lemaire is the smartest hockey man I've ever been around."

Lemaire was an important piece of the Montreal Canadien dynasty years, averaging 30 goals and 40 assists during his 12 years with the Habs, a time when the Canadiens dominated the game as few teams, in any sport, ever have. Perhaps of even more import to his players, he has won 49 playoff games and a Stanley Cup as a coach, and he brings that winning experience to the Wild.

"We know that this is only the first year," Lemaire said, pausing. He looked again at the current Wild roster posted on the wall and reflected for a few moments. "We know that four years from now there might only be seven or eight of these guys left, maybe ten, but we don't know. We really don't know. The thing is, every year if we are solid and we are moving up there will come a time when success will be right in front of us. And my goal is that!"

He made this statement with determination, and the glint returned to his eyes. There was a triumphant look that seemed to gaze into a future that has yet to unfold, saying, "Destiny is ours at some point, we are going to get it done." Lemaire can on occasion have a steely look that lets you know that he is talking seriously. It is a visible expression of the competitive nature of this champion. Notions of underestimating this man, if any ever existed, don't last long. After all, it was Lemaire who quickly built the New Jersey Devils into one of the top teams in the NHL, leading the team to the first 100-point season in franchise history in 1993-94, the year he won Coach of the Year honors.

Yet just as quickly, a gentler side emerges when he speaks, with a sense of resolve, about the leadership and goals that he hopes to provide for his squad. Lemaire is a man who wants the best for his young hockey team, but he wants the best for them as individuals, too. He believes in the improvement of the person as well as the player.

"It all goes hand in hand. If we follow the paths that I know will work, then we are going to a special place as a team. I want to bring discipline, caring for the team, you know? I want a family here in Minnesota." Lemaire was measuring his words as he spoke, and he looked me directly in the eye, his passion coming through quite clearly despite his thoughtful delivery.

"I really feel that the players on a team need to care for one another. It's all of these things, and that is what I feel can lead to success on the ice. As an example, even if I was to leave sometime, the foundation of this team will be strong going forward. That is how Doug Risebrough started things here, by hiring different guys who he feels can get the team to a strong position. We think the same way, as far as getting things done. When we were talking about the draft, we had the same ideas about what we need to do. About finding certain guys who might help us, especially on the power play."

Finding the right players to form the Minnesota Wild family would be the initial challenge for Risebrough, and making them a team would fall to Lemaire. The need to work together was obvious. "When we were molding this team, when Doug was putting a group of players together, he talked to me about different guys. He might say, 'Do you know this guy? What do you think of this player?' He wanted my input and was interested in my opinions.

"I know that when he talked to me at the beginning, he would say, 'You know, this guy might play better if he has a chance to play here.' What is really good is that Doug knows exactly the way I work, and with what he knows he has been able to bring in players who will fit with what I am trying to do."

Nearing the end of the season, it was abundantly clear the Wild had been fortunate to have an outstanding working relationship between the general manager and the coach. The Wild had won a lot of big hockey games by March, and had made the fans of Minnesota take notice of the connection between Risebrough and Lemaire and the on-ice success.

The two men were teammates on four championship teams in Montreal, and they share a vision as well as values. "That doesn't always happen, as I have seen many times. It's one of the reasons that you need to work with people you really know. You need to have a certain closeness between the GM and the coach or you may not end up in the same place. And I feel that is very important. When Doug acquires a player, he knows that player is going to fit with me, and would never say, 'Well, Jacques doesn't like that kind of guy, but I like him.'" Lemaire spoke very clearly for emphasis. "That does not often work. I think the way that Doug and I work together has been an advantage. If Doug knows that I don't like a certain player, I don't think he would bring him in here, because he knows that it needs to work with me, too."

Lemaire believes that a solid working relationship with his staff in New Jersey led to some great years there, and he finds some parallels between the two hockey organizations. "I enjoy the environment here for working and for playing hockey. I appreciated New Jersey too, certainly. There were great people on board over there." He glanced at his folded hands, perhaps having a Stanley Cup memory. "When I was with Larry Robinson and Jacques Caron, well, I really loved it. Red Gendron was there at that time, along with a few others. It was a special time. The best part about being a coach of a champion is that you get to share the joy that the players are experiencing. We had success."

Lemaire shifted in his chair and returned to the present. "Now I feel like we are getting the same thing going here. Lou Lamoriello (New Jersey President and GM) was a person I was close to. I worked well with Lou in Jersey and here I am working well with Doug. I was close to Larry Robinson (current Devils coach and formerly an assistant under Lemaire), and here we have Mario Tremblay and Mike Ramsey. It's great to work with people with whom you get along, and it's also nice to have people you can count on. People who support you and want to get things done."

Lemaire has no use for blind loyalty, however. He wants his assistants to know that their individual contributions will be respected at all times. "They'll bring up things that I don't see, and I can recognize that what they want to try is better than what we are doing. I ask for input, and they come up with suggestions to make us a better hockey team. That's what it's all about. Whatever we can do to become a better hockey team, that's what Doug and myself and the rest of the staff want to make happen."

Jacques Lemaire glanced once again at the small board on the wall with his players' names, and quietly said, "My goal was to have a good start, a solid start as a new team and a new organization with new players. How could I not be happy with what these guys have given me? The effort has been there all the time, so I'm very proud of the guys. And I know Doug is, too."

FOUR

LET'S PLAY HOCKEY

"The thing about Jacques is the respect factor," said Darby Hendrickson early in the season. "He brings respect, he commands respect; it's a constant theme. There's very little garbage going on anywhere in his operation. I like the way he runs things and he doesn't seem to waste a word when he's teaching. He doesn't ramble on when he's talking to a player, so he brings a kind of efficiency to the practices as well as the games. It's very simple with him. When he's not happy he lets us know, but he's usually okay as long as we work hard. There have been times we've lost and he's said, 'I liked the effort; you were going for it, and that's what it takes.' We, as players, respect that.

"And he has a sense of humor. He might say, 'If you guys are going to practice so miserably, that's okay with me. I've got all day and I like being on the ice. It's fun to be here, so if you want a long, hard practice, we can arrange that.' A little dry humor, but our practices are consistently productive."

Jacques Lemaire introduced his understated method of communicating with players during training camp. He wasn't going to beat players over the head to get them to understand his system; they would need to work in practice, pay attention to his words and pick up on the lessons that he would patiently teach on the ice. But while he wanted to bring substance to the training and wanted to see his charges improve, Lemaire was not going to baby-sit players who didn't want to learn how to play hockey the right way.

"When you are trying to effect change in people, sometimes there is only a small window of time in which to make those changes," said Doug Risebrough. "I think what a lot of people miss is that they don't see that window soon enough, they don't capture that moment where the player is open to learning and to change. Jacques has a great way of intervening and bringing the message to the players.

"And he teaches," Risebrough added. "He simply loves to teach. I mean, the guy is out there with the players all the time. He did the same thing when he was a player, always working with the young guys on the Canadiens. He has great intuition and he sees things that others don't."

Jacques brings a warmth to his on-ice personality that isn't always present off the ice. There is an infectious joy that can be found when Lemaire is laboring in his element, teaching the game of hockey to his players. He puts his whole heart into the instructional process, working on detail for as long as it takes.

"A lot of coaches may make a point and then move on and don't really notice if you do it right the next time," said centerman Stacy Roest. "Jacques is not like that, in that he'll physically work with you until he thinks you've got it right. There's a lot of repetition if you're not catching on, and he tries to help a player understand why certain things are important. He's got a very hands-on approach."

Doug Risebrough thinks there is a reason for Lemaire's immersion in the details of teaching players to execute properly. "I think a lot of this comes from his experience in Montreal and the high esteem with which the veteran hockey players on the team were regarded, said Risebrough. "It's a part of that Montreal era in which we all came up; the veterans were important, and they took it upon themselves to help and to teach the young guys on the club. The Canadiens always had the largest staff in the league and they were the first team to go with assistant coaches, who worked primarily with the young players. That's a big part of the Montreal tradition and that is where a number of us come from.

"And you know what? That's the most fun you can have in coaching, working one-on-one with your players. Whatever happened the night before, whether it was good or bad, you can get out on the ice with them and get back to work. For the short time that I coached (with the Calgary Flames), that's what I remember being the most fun."

In a conversation before the inaugural season of the Minnesota Wild got underway, an NHL staffer preached caution. "They've brought in some tremendous hockey people to get this thing started, but I think you need to remember that it's going to be tough. When you form a new franchise by picking from the number 15 or 16 guys on the other teams, it's a little like trying to beat that guy's team with a group of pro hockey castoffs."

The gentleman had a point, and while visiting training camp practice at the Parade Ice Garden, I remembered his comments. Every team in the NHL was allowed to protect a certain number of players, which amounted to roughly 15 guys who were untouchable. The expansion franchises, the Columbus Blue Jackets and the Minnesota Wild, could then take turns picking players up off a huge board displaying the names of all the unprotected players. This "expansion draft" preceded the entry draft of eligible amateur players during the selection process at the Saddledome in Calgary, Alberta in June of 2000.

For the expansion franchises, forming a team was a little like playing poker in a game where your hand is what everybody else has discarded. When everyone at the table is done, what's left are the "cards" you must play with. Now place your bets and get on with the game. The fact that the Wild became a strong hockey team, in fairly short order, with players whose stock was down around the league, tells part of the story that emerged from the Xcel Energy Center during the Minnesota Wild's first year.

Major league hockey would semi-officially return to the state it had abandoned in 1993 when the puck dropped for the Wild's preseason home-opener against the Mighty Ducks of Anaheim on September 29, 2000. "The Exhibition opener is the another sign that hockey is reborn in our great state, and the first buds of the new franchise are blossoming," said Wild Chairman Bob Naegele, Jr. "The downtown area of St. Paul is in a period of reflowering and we are darn proud to be here."

The Ducks were led by coach Craig Hartsburg, a man who played his entire 10-year career with the Minnesota North Stars. Hartsburg was an excellent defenseman, scoring 98 goals and adding 315 assists for Minnesota while appearing in three All-Star games. He has nothing but good memories of playing hockey for the North Stars, and said he was glad to see hockey returned to his former home.

"The new building (Xcel Energy Center) is a great facility, and the fans are still a big part of the atmosphere, just like I remember. They will keep this place jumping throughout the year, I'm sure. I'm happy for the people who live in the Twin Cities, and the rest of the state, who missed having the NHL in their lives. It's back now, and it never should have left."

Wild Community Involvement

The staff and players of the Minnesota Wild have expressed a strong commitment to the community via their involvement in numerous civic efforts. This dedication as individuals and as a team was evident from the very beginning of the franchise, as the team wove itself into the fabric of the Twin Cities.

Marlene Wall, Community Relations Director for the Minnesota Wild, believes that a lot of the Wild's philosophy of giving stems from Chairman Bob Naegele, Jr. "His attitude has been that we couldn't make this whole thing a success without making the community our number-one priority," said Wall. Partners of the Wild, such as Wells Fargo, have also been strong players in reaching out to communities all around the state, touching thousands of kids' lives with their "Wells Fargo Wild Road Tour."

The Wild players and management have visited numerous schools and hospitals locally. The Wild served a holiday breakfast at the Dorothy Day Center in downtown St. Paul, where a variety of Wild personnel pitched in to create a day for the homeless. Players working the line included Jim Dowd, Aaron Gavey, Matt Johnson, Antti Laaksonen, Steve McKenna, Jamie McLennan and Wes Walz. And up the road, other players took their brand of Wild holiday cheer to Gillette Children's Specialty Heathcare. Wall notes that all Wild Players have contributed in a substantial manner, without exception.

Volume Services of America, in conjunction with the Minnesota Wild's 10,000 Rinks Program, announced that 157 non-profit organizations raised in excess of $600,000 during the first season. Youth hockey organizations from around the Twin Cities raised funds by selling programs and operating concession stands during Wild games. And "Wild About Youth," a program featuring former Olympic Gold Medal Winners Alana Blahoski, Neal Broten and Karen Bye, has fostered "grass roots" initiatives to build on the hockey tradition in Minnesota.

The Wild are heavily involved in "NHL Street," a league-wide street hockey program which provides local communities with street hockey equipment (sticks, balls, pucks, goals, and goalie equipment) at no charge. Kids receive instruction from local program centers, as well as playbooks and clinics, courtesy of the team. The goal of "NHL Street" is to provide kids, ages 6-16, an opportunity to learn and participate in the game.

Tough guy Andy Sutton revealed a softer side when he visited an "I Love To Read Month" event at Bailey Elementary School. While talking about his favorite books, he managed to take some time to talk about hockey. All in all, it was a great experience for the kids and for Sutton. "It's always fun to come out and interact with the kids," said Sutton. "It's nice if you can give any kind of positive message (to young people). You never know what you might say that will spark something in them."

The Wild looked good in the first official game in their new digs, winning 3-1 over the Mighty Ducks and showing the tough brand of defense that would become their trademark. "It's a preseason game, which means we're all trying to learn some things about players and their roles," said Hartsburg. "I think the Wild are going to be fine. They have a lot of speed up front, their defense is big and strong and they've got good goaltending. It's going to be tough to come back on them, especially in this building."

Mighty Ducks star Teemu Selanne, the high-scoring Finn who scored the lone Anaheim goal in the third period, was impressed by the arena and the people in the seats, announced at 18,516. "It was an awesome crowd, and the Wild were ready to play right away," said Selanne. "We were all watching what was going on with the fans and the players, which you can't do in this league. Everybody in the building was pumped up, and they did a great job of supporting their players. They've been waiting a long time for this."

The brand new arena passed its first inspection by the masses, despite the fact that finishing touches were ongoing. A few ladders were hidden behind partitions, and some floors and walls were in need of a little carpeting and paint. That didn't stop the flow of high praise for major league hockey's new digs. "This is an awesome place," said an obviously impressed 15-year-old Paul Anderson as he gazed toward the ice from the spacious lower concourse. "And the scoreboard; look at the size of that thing!"

Yes, the "Wildmation" matrix scoreboard is pretty amazing, displaying a lot of action and information in clear and concise pictures. But it was the sightlines that grabbed the attention of his dad. "There's not going to be a bad seat in the place," said Jim Anderson. "It reminds me of Mariucci Arena (home of the University of Minnesota hockey team) with the big bowl and fans close to the action." While we were talking, the Wild skated onto the ice for the very first time, in front of their expectant and appreciative fans. "This is going to be wild," said Paul, presumably with no pun intended.

The Xcel Energy Center has a distinctly open and airy feeling about it, created by the roomy yet surprisingly intimate environment. The facility does not have a mall or a warehouse feel to it, like some of the giant arenas that have been built in recent years. This is a place for hockey, first and foremost, although it will host well over 150 events a year: 43 Wild home games, concerts, family shows and the Minnesota State High School Hockey Tournament. The western end of the building has several gigantic windows, where a number of fans were found before the Anaheim game gazing out at the St. Paul Cathedral, the State Capitol and the city skyline. As people continue to explore the venue, they will come to the exhibits honoring Minnesota hockey and its great history, from high school to the colleges and the professionals. The "X" has a veritable shrine to high school hockey, where the state tournament is to hockey what Indiana's state tournament is to basketball. "It's a museum where they'll play hockey and have other events," according to Wild chairman Naegele.

With game time nearing, it was time to find the press box, which is on the same level as the ten-dollar seats. The lesser-priced seats are high above the ice, but they look down directly on the action. They offer excellent sightlines for the fan and a very unique upper deck experience. "It's almost like you're looking down through your feet," said Wild GM Doug Risebrough. "You can see what's happening anywhere on the playing surface."

The arena was filling to capacity for the evening's festivities, and the crowd was quick to embrace one of their own, Richfield, Minnesota local-boy-turned-Wild-centerman Darby Hendrickson. The place was really jumping during the introductions, and the crowd's enthusiastic roar became deafening when Hendrickson stepped onto the ice. Coach Jacques Lemaire was amazed at the presence of exuberant fans so near to his coaching realm. "They (the fans) were right there above us, and really loud," said Lemaire. "I thought maybe they were going to be coaching with me."

"It's an amazing thing to hear the appreciation the fans have for the return of hockey," said Hendrickson. "I'm just so happy to be a part of all the excitement." The fans' excitement was contagious and clearly inspired the play of the new home team, who brought the crowd to an ear-shattering crescendo by scoring three goals in the first period. Kai Nurminen notched the first just two minutes and 49 seconds into the game, followed by Brad Bombardir at 6:05, and Aaron Gavey at 10:46. The Wild were on their way to a victory, and the return of hockey was now a proven reality. Men on skates were playing NHL hockey in St. Paul, by golly, and while the regular-season home opener was still 11 days away, for those in attendance the fun had already started.

Those same Mighty Ducks of Anaheim would defeat the Minnesota Wild at the "Arrowhead Pond of Anaheim" by an identical score of 3-1 in the first-ever regular-season game played by the new franchise. Left Wing Marian Gaborik, the Wild's number-one draft pick in the 2000 NHL entry draft, tallied the first goal in club history at 18:59 of the second period with assists from Scott Pellerin and Jim Dowd. The Wild received a strong game from goalie Jamie McLennan, who turned away 36 shots in the loss, but the club couldn't capitalize on a 16-9 shot advantage in the first period. Matt Cullen, a Minnesota native who played at St. Cloud State, scored the game winner for the Ducks.

Following a 4-1 loss to Phoenix in their second game of the year, the Wild returned to St. Paul for their home opener. It was now time to kick things off for real, a regular-season NHL game at the Xcel Energy Center that would officially bring the league back to Minnesota. You knew this had to be a major event, because the Commissioner of the league, Gary Bettman, was in from New York, along with a bunch of movers and shakers from around the Twin Cities and the state. It was a hockey crowd with a touch of celebrity. Some Minnesota Twins and Vikings were spotted checking out the confines, while over by one of the concession stands the Governor of Minnesota,

Minnesotan Jeff Nielsen vs. Blackhawks.

Jesse Ventura, was shaking a few hands, as was his predecesor, former Governor Arne Carlson, who had worked very hard to make the new arena a reality. And a whole lot of smiling people were happily descending on the new hockey palace.

The joint went ballistic when Darby Hendrickson scored the first Wild goal at 17:19 of the first period. It became clear once again that the Xcel Energy Center was a building where the fans would be seen and heard, at high volume and at close range. "This place just goes crazy," said Scott Pellerin after the game. "When Darby scored, it got so loud I was checking to make sure all the rafters stayed in place. It was noisy during the exhibition games, but it's going to even more intense during the regular season. I'm sure not complaining. This is going to be a fabulous home building, and it will be tough for the other teams coming in here."

Hendrickson's goal came on a nice pass from Maxim Sushinsky, and Darby, on one knee, stuffed it home past a flailing Brian Boucher. The Wild took a 2-1 lead on a Marian Gaborik power play goal with a minute left in the second period, the Flyers tied it early in the third, and Minnesota took a 3-2 lead on a Wes Walz shorthanded score at 9:12 off a slick pass from Jeff Nielsen. Walz's goal was a sign of things to come, as he would finish tied for second in the NHL in shorthanded goals for the year (best ever by an expansion team player).

For a little under two minutes, it looked and felt like the Wild were going to steal their first victory, but Philly's solid (and offensive-minded) defenseman Eric Desjardins, who scored 55 points in 1999-00, tied the game for the Flyers with a one-timer from the point at 10:37. Manny Fernandez was forced to stay sharp in the overtime, stopping seven shots and turning away a couple of strong scoring opportunities to preserve the tie. The home opener was now under their belt, the Wild had aquitted themselves well, and it had been a splendid evening of NHL hockey.

"That was a special night," said coach Jacques Lemaire after the game. "We played pretty well and I think everyone who came had some fun. We didn't do too much in the second period (when the Wild were outshot 10-3), but we're going to get better. I'm satisfied with the way things went for the first game."

Hendrickson's goal had really ignited the place, and it was clear that the building and the fans were inspiring for him. "I can't tell you much about how it felt (to score the first goal) because there were a lot of strong feelings. I hope I get to experience that thrill a few more times, because it sure was fun! It was a great feeling, no doubt about that, and it's nice to pick up our first point (in the standings)."

Minnesota Wild scout and former North Star coach Glen Sonmor was the first person to tell me that the Wild offered some good possibilities for Darby Hendrickson. A lot of people have recognized, with the 20/20 vision of hindsight, that the Minnesota Wild was a good place for Darby to give his career a needed jolt, but it was Sonmor who turned to me in the Calgary Saddledome following the expansion draft and said, "I think he's going to get a full shot with this organization. This could be a good fit for Darby."

A few months later, Sonmor would upwardly revise his positive evaluation of the former Gopher. "He's a heckuva skater and turning out to be a whale of a player in the NHL. Some people around the league may have doubted him, but Darby never stopped believing that he could play at a high level, and he's the one who was right."

I remember having seen Hendrickson's name on the board at the expansion draft and staring at it for a few moments. There it was, midway down the board: from the Vancouver Canucks, Darby Hendrickson. The Richfield, Minnesota native and former University of Minnesota standout was coming home to play hockey in the NHL, along with his buddy, Golden Gopher and Grand Rapids sports star Jeff Nielsen. And now, here they were at the beginning of the season, working in St. Paul at the Xcel Energy Center and making a valuable contribution to the inaugural season of the Minnesota Wild!

Glen Sonmor: A Hockey Life

Minnesota Wild scout and former North Star coach Glen Sonmor is a class guy who has a smile and a kind word for almost everyone. A lot of those words involve hockey; hockey has been his life. He was the University of Minnesota freshman hockey coach back in the mid-1950's, the Golden Gopher varsity coach from 1966-1972, and then he got into the professional game with the Minnesota Fighting Saints. He was the head coach of the Minnesota North Stars for several years, which included that team's first Stanley Cup appearance in 1981.

Sonmor's claim to fame as a player might be that he was traded for Hall-of-Famer Andy Bathgate when Bathgate was just a kid. At the time, Glen was playing pretty good hockey for the Cleveland Barons of the AHL, the Ranger affiliate. The headline of the day was, "Barons trade Cannon for Pop-Gun." The inside joke is that Glen Sonmor was the "cannon" in the deal, while the future New York Ranger franchise player and Hall of Famer Bathgate was the "pop-gun."

Glen himself laughs uproariously at the memory of that accurate-at-the-moment news item, noting that "at the time, Cleveland didn't have any idea who the young Andy Bathgate was, and I was kind of a popular player in Cleveland." It didn't take long for Andy Bathgate to show the kind of player he was, eventually leading the New York Rangers in scoring for eight consecutive seasons en route to becoming an NHL hockey legend.

Sonmor's trademark was his gritty play at left wing, and he was shuttling between the Rangers and the Barons for a couple of years when he was seriously injured by a flying puck. The injury cost him his left eye. The date was February 23, 1955, and Cleveland was playing on the road at Pittsburgh. "I remember it clearly because I never lost consciousness. And my daughter had been born four days earlier," said Sonmor. "Emile Francis ("The Cat," as he was known, went on to become the longtime coach and general manager of the Rangers) was our goalie, and we were trailing in the game 2-1. I had scored our lone goal on a deflection from in close. We were in front of the Pittsburgh net again, battling for position, and the puck went out to the point. I was looking to score another goal and glanced out to look for the puck when, bang! the puck hit me in the left eye.

"I knew I was in trouble pretty much right away. One of the guys, my roommate, skated up and told me, 'You're going to be okay, roomie, it's just above the eye.' Then another player came over and said, 'It's gonna be all right, Glen, it got you just *below* the eye.' They were trying to make me feel better, but I had a sense that I'd been hit square in the eye. Ironically, it was a good buddy of mine who took the shot, a fellow named Steve Kraftcheck, and he felt terrible about the whole thing. We had played youth sports together in Hamilton, Ontario and I tried to reassure him a few times, over the years, that it was just one of those situations that can happen in hockey."

Stephen Kraftcheck died in 1997. A search through hockey records reveals a career professional hockey player who spent 16 years in the pro game, playing fewer than 150 games in parts of four seasons in the NHL. Most of those games came before the incident in Pittsburgh; after that, he played 11 more years of AHL hockey.

Glen had to make a major life adjustment, and he did. "I remember the doctor in Pittsburgh, a Dr. Rohm, coming in to my room after things had settled down a bit," said Sonmor. "He told me, 'Glen, your life is going to change now. You're not going to be able to play hockey again.' That was the end of my career as a player, but it was also the beginning of my career in coaching."

FIVE

THE WILD WAY

Having played five games, the Wild were still searching for their first victory. They had managed one tie to go along with four defeats and were facing the Tampa Bay Lightning on October 19th at the Xcel Energy Center. The Wild had played well in St. Louis the previous week but had come up empty, losing 2-0, and they had outshot Edmonton at home a couple of days later, losing 5-3. They had made some early challenges to put themselves in the victory column, but had fallen short.

It took a team effort to clinch the Minnesota Wild's first win in franchise history, a 6-5 squeaker over the Lightning. After falling behind 1-0 in the first period, Maxim Sushinsky put the Wild on the board less than a minute into the second with a power play score. Following Cam Stewart's first goal of the season at 13:12, Sushinsky would notch another power play goal at 15:05 to put the Wild ahead 3-2. Scott Pellerin's shorthanded goal to close the scoring in the second gave the Wild a 4-2 lead heading into the intermission, and they were looking, for the first time, like winners.

Tampa Bay fought back and closed to 4-3 on Todd Warriner's shorthanded goal 3:47 into the third period. The Wild failed to capitalize on a couple of scoring opportunities, and when Alexander Kharitonov scored with 5:33 remaining to tie the game, the once-boisterous crowd went silent. The Wild had surrendered a lead in the Edmonton game and never regained it, but this time it was the "Super Slovak," Marian Gaborik, netting two goals in the final 2:28 to finish off the Lightning. The victory celebration for the 18,064 fans pouring into the streets of St. Paul would now commence.

"I'm happy for the guys because we should've gotten this win before," said Wild coach Jacques Lemaire. "They've been working so hard, and the guys deserve a little chance to celebrate. I have to go home because there's practice tomorrow and another game in two nights."

During a late fall practice at the "X," Jacques Lemaire is doing some teaching. He's working with a couple of the Wild centermen, grabbing a stick and getting into position in the face-off circle. He's talking and moving around the dot, bouncing the stick on the ice, trying to make his point. Number 14, Darby Hendrickson, skates in to listen. He leans on his stick and tilts his head forward, checking in with the professor.

Lemaire feels that Hendrickson improved his draw play over the course of the season, to the Wild's benefit. "Darby was a little tentative at the start, but he picked things up quickly and became very reliable. I got more confident, watching him get better and more determined. Playing tough on the draw is an important part of getting things going on the offensive end."

John Russo of *Let's Play Hockey* magazine seconded the Wild coach, saying, "I think the thing that surprises me about Darby is the way he's been winning face-offs, and showing his character around the circle. He's awfully tough on the draw, going through his man on a number of occasions. He's worked hard on that part of his game, and it shows in the way he plays."

All the Wild centermen—Hendrickson and teammates Jim Dowd, Wes Walz, Stacy Roest and Aaron Gavey—are well respected for their work in the circle. Dowd notes that getting the players positioned correctly is a big part of the battle. "You need to get your guys lined up where you want them," says Dowd. "A lot of it is anticipation, and checking on the positioning of the other team. I look to see what my opponent may be trying to do, watching his hands and the way he is setting up. Is he looking to take the puck to the net, or is he simply trying to win the faceoff? Timing is the key, so you look for any edge you can get. Draws in the defensive zone can be the most important. Late in the game, during a close contest, they can be especially critical."

Dowd is a strong all-around player who may be the best passer on the team. Formerly a player on the New Jersey team coached by Jacques Lemaire, who calls him "Jimmy," Dowd knew what to expect when he came to the Wild. The quick centerman, who sat out a month with a rib cage injury and missed another four games with a neck strain, nonetheless finished the year 3rd on the team in assists. Up in the press box during his injury hiatus in January, he spoke of how his ribs "are making noises they're not supposed to make." When asked what he thought might be wrong, Dowd answered, "I'm not really sure. They aren't broken, but something really hurts."

Dowd was part of the Stanley Cup champion Devils in 1995, playing in more games in the playoffs (11) than he did during the regular season (10). He netted a pair of goals during the drive to the Cup, when he "made the most of the opportunity to play and scored a couple times. It was awful nice being a kid from New Jersey carrying around the Stanley Cup," recalled Dowd. "That has to be my biggest thrill in the game of hockey."

"Jacques always has a plan," observed Dowd during another evening in the press box. "He came to New Jersey talking about winning a Cup, and that year we lost to the (Pittsburgh) Penguins in the Eastern Conference finals. The very next year we won it. He really emphasizes team play, and that's what we have here; a lot of guys working together to make some good things happen."

Both Dowd and Hendrickson noted that you've got to have the players around you to make things happen on the face-off. "A good draw man is only as good as the players on the ice with him," said Hendrickson. "I try not to lose any face-off cleanly, because that can allow quick passing by the other team that leads to scoring opportunities." Added Dowd, "I never want to lose the puck cleanly off the draw. That can lead to the quick scoring opportunity that's hard to defend."

Stacy Roest finished the season first among Wild centers in face-off win percentage (56.6), though he didn't take nearly as many of them as the team leader, Wes Walz. Walz was on the dot a total of 723 times during the inaugural season. Roest had a slow start offensively for the Wild, and wanted to make contributions wherever he could. "Working hard in the circle was something I could contribute despite getting off slowly (Roest didn't notch his first goal until the fifth week of the season). There is a sense of being involved with the offense when you're taking the face-off."

Facing off with Mario Lemieux was the tough challenge the Wild centermen faced on February 11 at the Xcel Energy Center. Super Mario won 60 percent of his faceoffs in that game (16 of 26). Of course, guys like Lemieux who are outstanding in the circle tend to get tougher as the game progresses, becoming downright nasty when the game is on the line. Hendrickson considers Joe Sakic to be about as good as it gets on the dot. Bobby Holik of the New Jersey Devils is another player who is at his best during crunch-time, and the Great One himself, Wayne Gretzky, was always considered to be at his best when the chips were on the table, late in a close contest. Gretzky never had the league's best faceoff numbers for a full season, but he often won key draws at key times in key games.

Sometimes a center has to use his hockey stick like the swordsman Zorro, battling his opponent with the stick in a duel that may end when one of the wings comes in to steal the puck. Hendrickson views this kind of a stalemate to be a winning faceoff, as long as it's one of his guys, like Marian Gaborik or Antti Laaksonen, coming away from the circle with the goods.

"In different zones, you might try to do different things," remarked Hendrickson. "In the neutral zone, you want to win the draw if you can. In the offensive zone, you might want to 'lose' the draw to the corner, where forechecking can make it a good 'lose.' If the puck goes where you want it to go, that's a win, even though it might not show up that way on the stat sheet."

Lemaire has been generally pleased with the way his centermen (Walz, Hendrickson, Gavey, Roest, and Dowd) have handled things in the first year. "Its like everything we do here, though. We have to get better so we work hard on these things in practice. The harder we work, the better we'll get."

Darby Hendrickson values the contribution his father, Larry, has made to his chosen career, and recalled that he has been in skates since before he can remember. "My father taught me the game of hockey. I was in skates from the age of three, and was out on the ponds from about that time in my life. My brother Dan, who is a couple of years younger than I am (and a fine player who played professionally), was my buddy and we used to go out and play whenever we could as we grew up. That's what I remember the best, going to a rink to go skating on those cold nights in winter. Also, skating on the same line with my brother when we were in high school, and playing in the state tournament together, will always be favorite memories of mine, kind of an extension of our youth hockey experience.

"My dad was always supportive of our love of the game. He's always been a big influence on me as an athlete and as a hockey player. He taught me the game, and he's been a great help to me as my career moved forward. We talk a lot during the summer about what's going on in both our lives. We don't just talk about hockey stuff, either. We talk about family and some of the things that are really important in our lives. I hope his 'no surrender' attitude has rubbed off on me."

Dino Ciccarelli and Neal Broten were a few of the Minnesota players he met through his dad's work as strength and conditioning coach with the North Stars; meeting those guys probably rubbed off on him, too. Still, Hendrickson never really thought of himself as an extraordinary player as a youth. He just wanted to make the high school varsity in Richfield, Minnesota, his home town. "I knew I loved the game, but my expectations were pretty humble."

Then, after an exceptional junior year, and at the ripe old age of 17, he was drafted by the Toronto Maple Leafs in the 4th round. With his August birthday, Hendrickson barely slipped in age-wise for the draft, so he was eligible to be selected after that junior season (most players, if they are drafted out of high school, are taken after their senior year). But instead of taking Toronto's offer at that time, Hendrickson accepted a full ride to the University of Minnesota. He had a full year of high school hockey left and began to realize that there was a dream to pursue. There were several people who thought that he might someday play in the NHL, foremost among them his father and a Minnesota hockey legend by the name of Herb Brooks.

Larry Hendrickson speaks powerfully about the influence of Herb Brooks on Darby. Both the young skater and the maturing hockey player felt the presence of the once and future Olympic coach in his life. "Herbie" was a frequent visitor of the Hendricksons during his coaching tenure with the North Stars, and he enjoyed leading the numerous discussions on hockey that were a staple of the Hendrickson household.

During this time, Darby was continuing to work on his game. He played two years of college hockey at the University of Minnesota ("a phenomenal experience"), and went to the Olympics as a member of the United States hockey team. Hendrickson signed a contract with Toronto for a nice bonus after playing with the U.S. National Team during what would have been his junior year at the U of M, then participated in the 1994 Olympic games for the Red, White and Blue. He began his NHL career with the Toronto Maple Leafs later that year.

Wes Walz got a telephone call from Doug Risebrough during the summer of 2000, which he was enjoying out in British Columbia. When the phone rang and he heard Risebrough's voice on the other end, he was as surprised as could be, although the surprise was a pleasant one. Walz had not talked to the new Wild GM in several years, although he knew him from his years in the Calgary organization. Risebrough had been the GM while Walz was with the Flames, and to hear from Doug out of the blue had to mean that something was up.

At the time Risebrough called, Walz had spent the better parts of the previous four years playing hockey in Switzerland with Lugano of the Swiss Elite League. If Doug Risebrough was calling him at home, that had to mean hockey business, because he knew that "Riser" had been named the General Manager of a new NHL hockey franchise in Minnesota. When Doug asked him about the status of his contract in Europe, and whether he would be interested in playing again in the NHL, Wes Walz was excited.

Walz had been a professional hockey player since he was 17 years old and had played for four different NHL teams (Boston, Philadelphia, Calgary and Detroit), but he hadn't played in the league since the 1995-96 season when he played all of two games for the Red Wings, garnering exactly zero points. He spent the better part of that season with Adirondack of the AHL, and then moved on to Europe. Wes had just turned 30 years old and his pro hockey biological clock was starting to tick; if there was ever going to be a return to the NHL, this might be his final opportunity. A call from a GM he knew and respected was a call to be taken seriously.

In fact, Walz had his best year, by far, in the NHL while playing for Calgary in 1993-94. Although he started the season with Saint John of the AHL, he moved up to Calgary early in the year and played in 53 games with the Flames, scoring 11 goals and notching 27 assists for a career high 38 points. Additionally, his plus-minus rating that year was a tremendous plus 20. "Plus-minus" refer basically to the number of goals scored for (plus) and against (minus) a player's team while he is on the ice. Those numbers were outstanding for a man who played only 53 games for an average Calgary team. He was a legitimate NHL center with respectable numbers when he found himself battling some injuries and facing reduced playing time the following year. He was moved to Detroit for the 1995-96 season, didn't play much, and was sent to the AHL (Adirondack). The next year, he began his journey to Europe and played hockey in Switzerland. He would remain there for the next four years.

Then came the call from Risebrough.

"We were able to get together on the (salary) numbers to make me a part of the Wild organization pretty easily," said Walz. "I was excited about the prospect of playing in the league again, and the timing was right for me to give it another shot. The experience of playing in Switzerland had been a good one, but the challenge of living in Europe was growing a little tougher. My son needed to get started in school (Walz has two daughters as well), and the language barrier was becoming a factor in some of our decision-making. We were ready for a move."

In reality, it's very unusual for a guy to head to Europe late in his career and then return in style to the NHL. When a player goes to Europe, in most cases, that's the last you're going to hear of him. They play pretty good hockey in Europe, but it's not the NHL. Walz is appreciative of that fact, saying that "if it wasn't for expansion, who knows where I would be? If it wasn't for Doug Risebrough and the Wild, I might have ridden off into the sunset and never been heard from again."

The first few practices Walz had with the Wild, back at the inaugural training camp held at Parade Ice Garden, revealed some reasons why the lightning-fast center was able to make the jump back. He was as quick as anyone on the ice, and in the drills he showed himself to be able to handle and pass the puck with steady hands. He didn't waste any time getting off the blocks as far as scoring, either, putting the puck in the net with regularity during nonstop scrimmages.

Due to the extremely limited amount of time the team would have together before the start of the season, training camp was held at a frantic pace, and that worked to Walz's advantage. He has great hockey tools (he finished 3rd in the league in the skating contest that is part of the NHL Superskills Challenge, proving himself to be among the elite speed merchants in the game), and the fact that he arrived at camp prepared to bust his butt to get another chance at the NHL only helped him. He looked like one of the best players on the ice from the get-go.

"He's not a loud-spoken person, but he makes his statement on the ice," Jacques Lemaire said after watching Walz play well on an early season road trip. "He works really hard. He doesn't count the hours that he puts into this game; he stays in shape by pushing himself all the time."

It didn't take long for Jacques Lemaire to really connect with Wes Walz. Lemaire saw things in Walz that let him know that Wes was ready to learn and to improve—and to never, ever get outworked for the puck. No matter what else might happen, there was no way he was going to be outhustled. Lemaire began to speak highly of Walz early in the season, perhaps seeing something of himself in the 5' 10", 180-pound sparkplug: same size, same determined nature, same position. There are now different challenges in the NHL than Jacques had faced, certainly, but both men are competitors of the highest order.

Walz attributes his natural skating skills to his upbringing in Canada. Growing up, he hung out around the frozen rinks in Calgary and played a lot of hockey with his friends. He considers his Bantam coach, the late Rick Bailey, as the one person who most influenced his career, by motivating him to excel. Walz played a lot of outdoor hockey as a kid, and that's something he really loves about the move to Minnesota. "I get a chance to spend time with my son and skate a little in the out-of-doors. It's just like I remember, and I want to give him that experience, like my parents did for me. I think that's where most top players pick up their skills, playing outside with their buddies and developing a love for the game. That's how it was for me."

He would play big in the Wild's first-ever road victory, a 3-2 early-November win over the Calgary Flames in overtime. Walz, who hails from Calgary, potted a couple of goals against his former team while Jacques Lemaire recorded his 250th win as an NHL head coach. Walz would go on to play every game of the season for the Wild, along with Antti Laaksonen (who netted the game-winner in the Calgary win), the only players on the team to do so. Wes would go on to set an expansion team record for shorthanded goals with seven, which also placed him in a tie for second in the NHL in that category. The fleet face-off artist also finished tied for first on the club in goals (18), and first in takeaways (84) and face-offs won (723) for Wild.

The experience of playing for the Wild eventually moved Walz to feelings of gratitude for the brotherhood he feels toward the guys on his team. "It's been amazing how we have come together and developed a strong bond. I've never played on a team that has grown together like this one, and I feel very fortunate. We've accomplished a lot on the ice, and I think that's a reflection of the way we've shared this whole experience."

When Wes Walz became captain of the Wild for the month of December, it was the first time he had been captain of a hockey team since he was a 14-year-old boy in Calgary. "I wasn't very big when I was a kid, and being the team captain then didn't have anything to do with leadership. It was just a matter of who was scoring the most goals. This (becoming captain) is a huge honor, and certainly nothing I was expecting. I'm surprised and very humbled."

At the age of 30, Wes Walz was again a leading scorer on his team and not the biggest guy, but things were otherwise quite different for the new Wild captain. He followed Scott Pellerin in the captain's role, while Pellerin succeeded the first Wild captain, Sean O'Donnell. Lemaire decided to go with the rotating captain system after giving it a lot of consideration upon taking the coaching job with the team. Ultimately, the rotation of captains would be O'Donnell for October, Pellerin for November, Walz, then Bombardir for both January and February and Hendrickson from March through the end of the season in April.

It made sense for Brad Bombardir to become a captain of the team. "Bomber" is frequently the coaches' connection to the ice, and many directives are issued to the veteran defenseman. The fact that he remained captain for two months indicates a strong trust and respect for Bomber from Jacques Lemaire. He's not overwhelmingly big, though he plays larger than his 6' 1", 205-pound frame. He's a tough guy to push off the puck, and he's another guy (like Jim Dowd) from the New Jersey Devil system. He was there while Lemaire was coaching, and Jacques could get a pretty good read on Brad from seeing him play and getting some later insights from Lou Lamoriello. Jacques has a sense of trust in Bombardir.

Bomber has a way of getting in the way of the opposition's offensive thrusts, ranking first on the team and eighth in the NHL with 164 blocked shots. The 70 games that he played in were a career high (despite fighting a severe groin strain during October and back spasms in March), as were his 15 assists, including three in the November 18 victory over Boston. He's a winner, having been a member of the 2000 New Jersey Devils Stanley Cup champions, and Bombardir was indeed the first (and only) Wild player to wear the captains "C" for consecutive months. (Hendrickson was captain for March and kept the "C" until the end of the season on April 8.)

When the Wild name their monthly captain, it is announced in the press release as a decision made by "Minnesota Wild GM Doug Risebrough and coach Jacques Lemaire," but it was really Lemaire's idea to select a different captain for each month. The monthly rotation was a tool that he felt would increase the sense of responsibility that selected players would have for the team. Players were chosen for their leadership qualities, and by rotating captains, he would be building that many more leaders for the future. Lemaire likes what he has seen from his captains thus far, and he says he may stick with the system as long as he is behind the Wild bench.

A former NHL coach spoke of having "that one special guy who leads by example. When you have that kind of guy, you want to keep him in the captain's role." In that regard, it makes sense for Lemaire to rotate the job, because the Wild are a new team with no established leaders; it's not like Detroit, where Steve Yzerman enters his 16th year as the Red Wings' captain, or Colorado, where Joe Sakic will wear the "C' for a 10th year.

"I'm very happy with how this (the captain rotation) has worked," said Jacques later in the season. "All of the guys have worked extra hard when they took their turn, which is why I wanted to try it. Sometimes you have a veteran who is the captain, and it is very hard to take the "C' away from him once he has it. About the only way you would be able to change that would be to trade him, or perhaps you might get lucky and he would retire," he said with a smile.

Twin Cities sports journalist Eric Nelson was talking about the killer instinct the Wild showed in the Boston Bruins-Minnesota Wild contest played November 18th at the Boston Fleet Center. "That was a game that you can't ignore, in terms of going on the road and pounding a team that was quality, or certainly has the tradition of high quality."

Yes, the Bruins at the Boston Garden carried a grand tradition, but on that night at the Fleet Center these Bruins were a step slow for their new coach Mike Keenan. Keenan is well known for playing mind games to motivate his troops, and has been called by some the toughest coach in the NHL to play for. How else could one explain the Wild clicking on four power play goals after starting the season 0-for-46 with the man advantage on the road? It seemed as if maybe it was vintage "Iron Mike," hanging his players out to dry to let them know that they needed to listen to the tough taskmaster now at the helm. Or perhaps it was simply the Wild coming together at the expense of Keenan's charges.

Whatever the reasons, the Saturday-night game was a crescendo of Wild scoring: one goal in the first period, two potted in the second, and three more in the third. Max Sushinsky started off the big night, scoring with the help of some slick passing from Scott Pellerin and Darby Hendrickson. Lubomir Sekeras then got a pair back-to-back in the second, using his booming slapshot to twice beat Bruins netminder Byron DaFoe. In the third, Sushinsky got his 6th of the season, while Hendrickson and Peter Bartos closed out the scoring. The Bomber, Brad Bombardir, was huge in the game with three assists. Eight days earlier the Wild had thumped Chicago 5-2, but this result against the Bruins was a nice numerical reversal of a 6-1 loss at Toronto in late October, the Wild's worst loss of the year.

Things were starting to look a little different for the men from Minnesota. In their first six road games of the young season, the Wild had scored a *total* of six goals in five losses and a tie. In the following five road appearances, including a 2-0 shutout loss to Colorado and Patrick Roy, Minnesota scored 15 goals in winning three games and losing two. Things were starting to gel a little on the offensive end, with the flow of goals a result of practice and patience, according to Scott Pellerin.

"It seems like we're getting to know each other better, and it's starting to show. We keep working and it feels like there's been some progress on the offensive end. Hopefully, we'll be able to keep it going," said the Wild left wing.

By the time of the Boston game, the Wild had been playing together as a team for just over two months. They had started literally from scratch and were just now showing significant progress. Two months is not a lot of time for a new professional team, in any sport, to show notable results, but the Wild finally had some real fun and it came at the expense of the Bruins. "That was the first time during the year that I really felt good about the way we played. I came out of that game smiling for the first time this season," said Jacques Lemaire. "We played well as a team and put the puck in the net a few times."

There wasn't a lot of smiling going on in the other locker room. Words like "humiliating" and "frustrating" were being tossed around, although the acquisition of Bill Guerin (a Massachusetts native) from Edmonton was being viewed in Boston as a positive by the fans and media. That same New England jury was still deliberating on the pick-up of hockey's stoic survivor, Mike Keenan, to replace Pat Burns, fired early in his fourth year behind the Bruins bench.

There must have been a realization on the part of the discerning Boston crowd, who ended the game against the Wild by cheering (amidst catcalls) the goals by Hendrickson and Bartos, that a turn to Keenan was a sign of a desperate need to move quickly to save the season. Perhaps there was some genuine admiration for the visitor's effort, but there was anger and sarcasm as well. A 6-1 hammering of the once-legendary Boston Bruins, home of Bobby Orr and Phil Esposito and 23-year veteran John "Chief" Bucyk on their own ice, not by a Colorado or Pittsburgh or New Jersey, but at the hands of this expansion team? There could be no greater embarrassment.

Keenan appeared calm after the game, saying that there would be better days ahead. It seemed like a set-up game for the intense brand of coaching sure to come from this master manipulator, perhaps a mental clearing of the decks that would hopefully lead to the required attitude adjustment. There is danger in such strategy, but Keenan has been known to fall back on the whip if psychological efforts fail. While Keenan was in Chicago, from 1988-1992, after a similar effort at resuscitation, a key Blackhawk player said, "you can only beat a horse for so long before it eventually quits on you. It seems like we're always being pushed and pushed and pushed."

Keenan is a complex man, capable of explosions of temper that intimidate and befuddle players. The storied whip had not yet been applied to these Bruins. There was hope in Boston that Keenan was continuing the development he had shown during the 1993-1994 Stanley Cup season with the New York Rangers, when he had given, in the words of Mark Messier, the "most powerful, most intense, most emotional speech" he had ever heard in 16 seasons, right before game seven of the Rangers' Stanley Cup final with Vancouver.

Keenan would survive the balance of the 2000-2001 season, but the Bruins would finish one exasperating point out of the playoffs. If Boston had emerged victorious in just one of their four meetings with Atlanta, one of the worst teams in the league, they would have made the post-season. They didn't, and despite some big wins late in the season, Mike Keenan was forced out as coach of the Bruins at the year's end.

The contrasts between a coach like Mike Keenan and one like Jacques Lemaire are stark. Lemaire refuses to play the emotional chords that sometimes work for Keenan. His is a much more subtle manner of leadership—though make no mistake, strong leadership it is. For Lemaire, the joy of the game is in letting the guys discover themselves as hockey players through his teaching and their own hard work. Meaningful practice is essential for Jacques Lemaire, to instill consistent discipline. He doesn't scream or manipulate if a man doesn't hustle on the ice; that player will simply be invited to sit down and watch some hockey from the bench, or perhaps to go play hockey at a different location, like a minor league. Keenan and Lemaire are two men at opposite ends of the coaching spectrum, yet interestingly, each has produced a Stanley Cup title, one after the other: Keenan in 1994 and Lemaire in 1995.

By late November Jacques Lemaire had proven capable of convincing his team that the system would win for them if they would believe in it. That's not always easy to accomplish in the NHL, though it no doubt helped him to have a new team whose players were willing (and in most cases, *eager*) to listen. Lemaire makes a priority of treating his players like men, but if they don't respond to his message it will be difficult, if not impossible, to endure in his system. The players have to be ready to play, and the coaching staff will do all that it can to enable their top performance. "We ask the guys to play with intensity at all times", said Lemaire following a November practice. "It's the coaches' job to get the right players going at the right time, to put them in situations where they can have success. I like the way my guys work in practice."

Assistant coach Mike Ramsey is a tough, bright guy who played the game at the highest level the right way, the kind of assistant coach a major league player can respect. Not only is Ramsey an intelligent man who relates well to the team, he's a guy who doesn't waste words when he speaks. Says Hendrickson, "Mike has a way of teaching, of coaching that is calm in manner. It's easy to listen to a guy like that, especially when he backs it up with a 17-year All-Star type career. He's a lot like Paul Molitor (former All-Star player and current coach of the Minnesota Twins) in that regard, I would guess."

Ramsey is a Minneapolis, Minnesota native who did enjoy an extraordinary playing career that included participation in four NHL All-Star games. He was also a member of the 1980 U.S. Olympic hockey team, which stunned the world by defeating the Soviet Union in the "Miracle on Ice" game at Lake Placid, N.Y. "That was an amazing experience," said Ramsey, who was recently elected to the U.S. Hockey Hall of Fame.

Wild assistant Mario Tremblay also enjoys working out with the boys during practice and putting some of his old Montreal moves on the Wild goaltenders. When he began playing for the Canadiens in 1974, at age 18, he became the youngest player ever to wear the Montreal Canadiens sweater. He still enjoys scoring during the one-on-

one drills with the goaltender, as well as providing some entertainment for the players during practice. He's lost a step, perhaps, but he still looks like a natural on the ice as he glides toward the net. "Mario is a little more animated, but it's the same type of deal with all the coaches; they know their stuff and they've both been there, so maybe you listen a little closer. You can learn a lot from those guys," says Hendrickson.

We've all heard the popular expression, "Those who can't do it, teach." Well, that's not the case with the Minnesota Wild staff. Jacques Lemaire, Mario Tremblay and Mike Ramsey have been there and done that, as exemplified by their extraordinary careers, and it has to help a young squad to be immersed in such high-quality coaching on an everyday basis. The coaches are out there skating with the guys all the time, working to improve the Wild players with on-ice teaching. That's the "hands-on" manner of instruction that the players get to benefit from.

Despite all of his contributions to the Montreal Canadiens, Jacques Lemaire was never chosen for an All-Star team. This was largely due to competition at the center position during his 12-year career, and to the fact that he was a low key, quiet individual who never demanded attention. Both teammates and opponents felt he was under-rated. "He was always a big presence in games that he was in," said Wild scout Glen Sonmor. "Jacques was a fabulous player. I think the most telling statistic regarding Lemaire is that he was the leading scorer in his final Stanley Cup playoffs, and then he retired. He was only 32 years old, still a great player, obviously, and he walked away from playing the game on his own terms. That says a lot."

The Wild played a solid game against the Vancouver Canucks on November 26, a contest that would result in the Wild's unbeaten streak reaching four games, including back-to-back wins. Before this stretch that began with the Boston game, the club's longest unbeaten string was a very humble two games—both ties. By defeating the Canucks 4-2, the Wild had recorded their most impressive victory of the season. Their previous victories were against Chicago (twice), Calgary (twice), Boston and Tampa Bay, none of whom were considered to be the quality of the Canucks

Vancouver has a strong team and came into the contest playing good hockey, having won four of their last six while compiling a record of 12-6-3-2 overall. "That's a good team over there," said Jacques Lemaire after the game. "They have a lot of good players." The Wild grabbed a three goal lead on two goals by Laaksonen followed by Wes Walz's shorthanded tally. That lead was cut to 3-1 on a goal by prized Vancouver rookie Daniel

Sedin (who, along with brother Henrik, are highly regarded twin brothers from Sweden) at 13:48 of the second, and that was the score heading into the second intermission.

Manny Fernandez got a little careless at the beginning of the third period, and Robbinsdale, Minnesota's Trent Klatt took advantage by swooping in and firing the puck past Fernandez with just seven seconds gone in the third. It was a difficult goal for Manny to accept ("Some kind of a poor play on my part," Manny said later), and it seemed to put the Canucks back in contention. They were applying steady pressure in the third, outshooting the Wild 12-6 for the session, when Antti grabbed a nifty pass from Ladislav Benysek and pushed it past Vancouver goalie Felix Potvin for a 4-2 advantage and a hat trick for Laaksonen (or *Hattutemppu* in Finnish), the first-ever Minnesota Wild player to accomplish the feat.

The win was a big one, but Antti Laaksonen was the story of the evening as his third goal sent a wide variety of hats cascading to the ice. There was joy in the air at the "X" following the victory, while Jacques Lemaire maintained his typical cool after the game. "Antti is playing very well for us, and we did a few things right today. For me, it's more important how we are playing and improving than the wins or losses. I like to win, of course I do. Maybe if we get a streak of five or six, then I'll start to care about it more."

That would come a few weeks later.

THE EUROPEANS

Consistency is usually not a watchword for rookies in the league, but Marian Gaborik played tough night in and night out, with points in seven straight games (five goals, four assists) between January 17 and February 6, 2001. That tied him for the longest streak of the season among NHL rookies, and was a big part of the Wild's 5-1-1 record during that stretch.

Even coach Jacques Lemaire was surprised by Gaborik's immediate success. "You're talking about a very young player who had some good talent but had a lot to learn. He needed to see what he had to do in the defensive end because he was used to the more wide-open European game. He listens to the coaches, most of the time," said Lemaire, smiling, "and he's going to be a good hockey player if he keeps working on the things we are telling him."

Gaborik appears to have the Lemaire mantra of playing good defense well in mind. "It's important that I play good defensively to clear the puck out of our zone," said Gaborik after scoring the second goal of the game, and his 17th goal of the season, during the 3-3 tie with St. Louis in early March. "That's important to getting the puck going the other way, and I can use my speed to make a rush on the offensive end."

Gaborik excels on the open ice and scored several of his goals on breakaways. He has an exquisite sense of timing and enough afterburner speed to clear defenses in an instant. His great hands allow him to hold the puck until the last moment, often forcing the goalie into the first move. That is usually all it takes for the hyper-quick winger to stuff it home.

There is growing concern in some North American circles that Canadian influence in hockey is on the wane, or at least in a mild decline. Yes, hockey still reigns supreme in Canada, and Darby Hendrickson experienced the hockey mania north of the border while playing for the Vancouver Canucks and the Toronto Maple Leafs. Nevertheless, it is a fact that Canadians no longer dominate the game from a numbers standpoint as they once did.

"There's a strong international influence in the game today," said Hendrickson. "I think it has made the league more competitive than it has ever been, and raised the intensity level accordingly. Nowadays, you're likely to see these guys in a World tournament or at the Olympics, and I think the rivalries grow. I know they do."

Hendrickson has tremendous respect for the Canadian love of their national game. "The Canadians have been great at hockey forever, and hockey in Canada is like baseball here, in the sense of its being the national pastime. Even more so. I think they are reassessing their game somewhat as the influence of the Europeans, the Czechs and Slovaks in particular, expands. There may be a sense of wanting to stay on top of the world stage as the game continues to grow globally."

There's been a Russian movement for some time, and a number of great players have come over from Russia and the former Soviet Union, some truly outstanding players. You think of some of the great Russian players, and you have to think of the Detroit Red Wing teams of the 1990's, with names like Sergei Fedorov (who played in 129 playoff games for the Wings), Vyacheslav Kozlov, Igor Larionov and Viacheslav Fetisov.

Lately, it seems, the trend is that the Czechs and the Slovaks are coming up with the outstanding players. Where they come from seems like a good question, because we don't know their system and therefore we don't expect players from that part of the world to be so good, but they are. They certainly don't have the hockey tradition of Canada, but they are producing outstanding players, like Marian Gaborik of the Wild, who hails from Trencin, Slovakia. Many come from the industrial sections of urban areas as well as from rural towns that used to be off the "bird dog" scouts' beaten track; in either case, youth hockey is played far from the glamour of the NHL.

Most of the young players who have success in the former "eastern bloc" countries are gritty kids looking to excel in a tough game. The rinks are few and far between, and they play on wider ice sheets that promote an offensive style of play. And now the Russians seem to be strengthening their amateur game again, as exemplified by the 2001 entry draft, when three of the first five players drafted came from Russia. There has been concern about economic decay and poor outside influences on young players in Russia, but the bottom line seems to be that great players will continue to come from that nation.

Marian Gaborik can play hockey. The 6' 1" 185-pounder from Trencin, Slovakia was the Minnesota Wild's first-ever selection in the 2000 NHL entry draft (the third pick overall). He may have just turned 19 in February of 2001, but his youth doesn't matter. Gaborik can flat out play hockey, has matured quickly, and is learning to play the game by NHL standards using speed, finesse and a large amount of guile. He's the Stealth Slovak, a hard-charging skater who looks for any opportunity to make his quick, darting moves through traffic and advance toward the goal. Marian Gaborik is the hockey equivalent of "the Natural."

Gaborik can play the game well at its highest level, although he is still learning the

Antti Laaksonen gets his "hattutemppu" (Finnish for "hat trick").

language and works harder to explain his success than to achieve it. "When I come in on the net, I like to try and find a place that the goalie can't protect. Sometimes he will make a move, and then I find the spot where I can shoot." It sounds simple, but, of course, scoring goals in the NHL is a tougher proposition than he makes it sound. Gaborik, a member of The Hockey News all-rookie team in 2001, is one of those rare hockey players with the ability to make the game look easy.

Mike Ramsey, the Minnesota Wild assistant coach, is impressed by Marian's offensive hockey gifts. "He's got a goal scorer's hands. He scores goals that you might say were lucky—batting pucks out of the air, scoring on the backhand while going away from the net. If he's tied up he finds a way to get his stick free so he can get a quick shot on net. But the fact is you see good goal scorers doing that every time you watch the highlights. It's the same guys whacking those goals in and they don't score by accident."

Tommy Thompson had the job of making a final determination on the skills of Marian Gaborik before the 2000 entry draft. To do so, he watched Gaborik closely a number of times while he was on the ice, and also evaluated him off the ice. "We particularly liked Marian," says Thompson. "We had seen him for the first time two years ago at the World Junior Championships in Winnipeg. It's very difficult for a 17-year-old to play well in that tournament, and Marian did extremely well as a 16-year-old.

"We followed him closely and saw him play in all sorts of situations. We saw him with his team at the World Juniors, we saw him in a number of games in the elite league in Slovakia and we saw him play with his national team against the national teams of other European countries. We visited with his family, talked to Marian and got to know him very well."

Gaborik is not the first hockey player to come from the Trencin area of Slovakia. Other quality players have come before him to the NHL, including All-Star caliber players Pavol Demitra, Marian Hossa, Ziggy Palffy and Miroslav Satan.

Rick Dudley, the Tampa Bay Lightning GM, understood the Wild's decision to select Gaborik at the 2000 entry draft in Calgary. In fact, Dudley stated that if he had owned the first pick, he would have undoubtedly taken the speedy Gaborik. "We had Gaborik rated number one in the draft, without question. This kid's just a great talent. We were hoping we'd win the draft lottery. If we had, Gaborik would be skating for the Tampa Bay Lightning today. He's got great speed and a great release. He can score and he can make a play."

Although Gaborik never scored against the Phoenix Coyotes in the four contests the two teams played in 2000-01, he impressed head coach Bobby Francis with his quickness and his uncanny ability to move through traffic. "I think he has the skills to be something special," said Francis. "The first time we played Minnesota, he did an end-to-end rush that reminded me of Gilbert Perreault. He has the ability to cut through the trap like a hot knife through butter."

When the Wild went to camp, the general sentiment was that Gaborik would start the season in the IHL, and perhaps work his way onto the big club. That, of course, is not how it went. The Wild needed players who could put the puck in the net, and Gaborik quickly established himself as just that type of offensive threat. Skating at the Parade Ice Garden during camp, onlookers couldn't help but notice the skills possessed by the number one draft pick. The kid could skate, he had great hands and he could score. How do you keep a player, who is clearly one of the most talented guys in camp, down on the farm? Wild scout Glen Sonmor said, "I know they didn't want to start him up here, but how are you going to send him down?" In the end, the Wild brain trust found they needed to use the exceptional Slovakian on the big club.

Gaborik scored the first regular season goal in Wild history in his first NHL game at Anaheim (the youngest player ever to score an expansion team's first goal), and finished the season ranked first on the Wild in points (36) and shots (179), and tied for

first in goals with 18. He also scored in the Wild's inaugural regular-season home game, the first power play goal in the new arena, during the second period of the game with Philadelphia. Marian Gaborik was an impact player from the very start of his NHL career.

"We certainly thought that Marian Gaborik was one of the most skilled players in the draft," said Doug Risebrough shortly after the Wild selected him. "He is an outstanding skater and has proven to be a prolific scorer in both the Slovakian league and in international play. We look forward to having him in our organization for many years."

Risebrough appreciates the way that Gaborik has risen quickly to become a

"Krivo"

major force on the Minnesota Wild hockey club, but is mindful that the process is ongoing.

"The key for us, from a management perspective, is that this is about long-term development," commented the Wild GM during the summer of 2001. "We feel we were lucky last year with Gaborik. We expected Marian to work up the ladder through the minors to the NHL level, and that just didn't happen. It was the opposite with him. He was a good player for us all year, and that's because he worked hard and committed to the little things in his game, and ultimately won a spot on the team. We're not anticipating that will happen again. We would be happy if it does, but we're not expecting it."

Tommy Thompson echoes Risebrough's thoughts, saying: "We always want to make sure a young guy is really ready before he makes that next step. I've told a couple of our prospects for 2001-02 that if they come to training camp expecting to make the team, they've got to force their way onto the hockey club. That's what Marian did last year; he forced his way into the line-up. Remember, too, that Gaborik played with men for a couple of years in the Slovakian league. That helped him."

Gaborik played at a high level for two seasons with Dukla Trencin of the Slovakia Senior League, where he scored 37 goals and notched 31 assists in 86 games. Most importantly, he gained from the experience of playing with older, more seasoned players who would not take it easy against the young phenom. He would get banged around by the big boys, which furthered his development into a player wise beyond his years. And

Filip Kuba plays tough for the Wild.

that experience helps Gaborik to use his speed more effectively, to know when to turn it up a notch when there's an opportunity. Gaborik has a "fifth gear" that he can use to separate himself from a defender.

Gaborik played in 71 games in his first NHL season, missing 10 games due to injury. He suffered a leg contusion that caused him to miss six games at the end of November, and an abdominal strain that forced him out of the last four games of his rookie campaign. When he injured the leg against the Rangers at home, there was some concern that Gaborik was being targeted by other teams. On two occasions Ranger players flew at Gaborik, alarming coach Jacques Lemaire. "There is no reason for other players, especially veterans, to be taking cheap shots at Marian. He should have the respect of the older players in the league. Players like him are the future of the league."

Mike Ramsey brings his 18-year career as a player in the NHL to his role as coach of the Wild's defensive players. "I think it helps, when the players get in certain situations, for a coach to know what's going through their minds," said Ramsey. "I've been in just about every spot that they're going to face out there. I enjoy the teaching challenges that come with coaching young players, as well as players who are new to a system. It's been especially rewarding here."

Ramsey appreciates the fact that he is working for one of the best teachers in the game in Jacques Lemaire. "A lot of coaches around the league will tell a player what to do, but Jacques teaches guys how to play the game. There's a big difference between the two styles of coaching, and we're trying to instill confidence while educating the player," stated one of the newest members of the Buffalo Sabres Hall of Fame.

He's had his work cut out with some of the young guys who inhabit the Wild defensive corps, hungry players who make mistakes but are eager to learn. "I don't get disappointed in our young guys, as long as they work hard and keep learning. Sure, everybody would like to see a Ray Bourque or Al MacInnis quarterbacking things, but that's not fair to a young guy like Filip Kuba, who is going to improve and has a lot of potential."

Kuba has played like a man possessed in his effort to earn respect in the NHL. During the 1999-00 season Kuba spent part of the year with the Florida Panthers before he was sent to Houston of the International Hockey League. The 6' 3", 210-pound defenseman had just one goal and five assists with Florida and was listed in the Wild Team guide as a player "in the system," which means he was far from assured of a place on the roster.

He's come on like gangbusters for the Wild. Kuba finished the season having played in 75 games, scoring nine goals and adding 21 assists. Ten of those assists were on the power play and he finished with 14 power play points. "I only played in 13 games for Florida," said Kuba, who is from Ostraba, Czech Republic. "I'm getting a chance to play here and to prove that I belong in the NHL. This has been very good for me, playing for the Wild."

Ramsey says he has enjoyed working with the Europeans who have been a large part of the Wild defense. The guys who are affectionately referenced as the Czech "mob" have proven coachable and, Ramsey points out, good hockey players. The Czech and Slovak players like to hang out together, going to movies and having dinner with one another, their language naturally being a common bond. The good-natured ribbing that takes place at practice reveals the affection that the guys have for one another, with Sekeras and Ladislav Benysek in key roles.

"Benysek is one of the leaders of the group (there were four Czech and two Slovak players on the Wild's season-ending roster), a strong physical player who should keep improving his head for the game," said Ramsey. "I think he has a lot of upside potential and he's a good guy to have around. Most people don't recognize the kind of skater he is, probably one of the fastest people on the team. He was very close on a few offensive opportunities and could have scored a little more. I think he's going to get over the hump as an NHL player in the future. And Ladislav is still a fairly young guy (26 in 2001)."

Benysek, who sometimes plays the role of translator, was thinking about becoming a lawyer until he was drafted by Edmonton in 1994. Strong play at the World Championships earned him another shot at the NHL after playing just two games with Edmonton and returning to the Czech Republic. One cold winter day, after practice, he was talking about how the Twin Cities were "very nice, and it must be very good in the summer. I like to bicycle and can't do it now." No, it's probably not a very good idea for a pro hockey player to negotiate the slippery roads of Minnesota on a bike in the dead of winter. But the man from the beautiful city of Prague, Czech Republic, does appreciate life in the NHL and wants to keep working on refining his hockey skills. "It's good to be on this kind of a team. There are a lot of good guys who have helped with the adjustments we have to make. It's a very different game over here, with the smaller rinks and much more physical play. It's faster, too, with every player a good player.

"I like playing the best players on the ice, and that's why most guys come over here. The best in the game play in the NHL, so we come."

Sometimes it pays to be lucky rather than good. Or, it can really pay to be a little bit of both. Such was the case with the 32-year-old rookie sensation with the slapshot, Lubomir Sekeras.

"With Lubomir, I hate to admit the amount of luck that we had," recalled Doug Risebrough. "We were trying to acquire late draft selections at the end to pick up a few veteran players, because we thought they might have a shot with us. When it came right down to it at the draft table, we had to make a decision between a younger guy and an older guy (Sekeras). Pierre Page, who was making the recommendation, liked both of the players but thought we should take the young guy."

So Risebrough was left with a dilemma, and he admits he wasn't certain what decision to make even as he made it. Finally, he decided to take the older player because, as the thinking goes, he might fit better into the situation. Perhaps he could bring a little personal maturity into the "foreign environs" of the Minnesota Wild camp, even lend a little experience to the European presence. That player was Lubomir Sekeras.

"So we made the selection, and I figured old meant 27 or 28," Risebrough says as he starts to laugh. "And then when I asked just how old he was, somebody said, 'You know, he's 32'. And I kind of did a double-take."

Doug began to roar with laughter as he recalled the comical moment at the normally staid draft table. "Now, if I had known that 'old' meant 32 years old, which *is* old in this game for a new player, I'm sure I would have taken the younger guy."

He paused and glanced across the table with a big grin, like a man with a punch line to deliver. "So Jacques, who's sitting at the table on the other end from me, finds out how old this draftee is and walks over and says, with a funny look on his face, 'Doug, nobody older than me, please!'" Risebrough laughed again at the hilarity of the moment. "Nobody older than me, please." The Wild GM shook his head at the memory.

For various reasons, Lubomir was late in signing a contract and thus was late in getting to camp. When he did show up, Risebrough was not immediately impressed. "We knew that he was going to show up one day, and sure enough I get to the rink for practice and here's this guy sitting in the corner looking tentative," said Risebrough. "I turned to my assistant and I said, 'Don't tell me, *please* don't tell me that's Sekeras.' Yep, sure enough it was Lubomir. And I thought to myself, perhaps we should just send him home right now.

"He sure didn't look like he was going to be able to shoot a puck 100 miles per hour. Turns out he's got a great shot, he's a competitor and he has an infectious personality. He doesn't speak a lot of English, but in some ways I think he became a rallying point for the team. We now realize he's a great guy and a very good hockey player. That's a great punch-line; to have your disappointing draftee turn out to be a strong contributor with arguably the hardest slap-shot on the team."

One day, while waiting for practice to end so I could have a word with Sekeras (he spoke very little English), I watched Lubomir stay late, by himself, rifling pucks into the net. He was doing this very informal exercise from center ice, simply firing slappers one after another at the unattended goal. He must have stroked about ten consecutive shots into the center of the net, at high velocity, before doing a quick half-lap around the ice and disappearing into the locker room. It was a darned impressive display of shooting skills; to this day, I don't think he knew that anyone was watching him as he raised his arms in triumph after every few shots, like a victorious heavyweight after the bout.

The Wild players have an affection for "Lubo." Darby Hendrickson tells a story about working out one day and finding Sekeras singing into one of his exercise barbells. Here's Lubomir rocking and rolling with the barbell in the weight room, air-singing along with a little Van Halen as though the weight was a microphone. "He's a character in some ways," says Hendrickson, "but he's a nice part of this hockey team."

Sekeras is working on his English-speaking skills, and he did have some success in that department as the season progressed. After the 6-0 rout of Dallas, during which he netted the fifth goal of the onslaught, he was asked about a dry spell in goal scoring that extended back to his two power-play goals against Boston in the 6-1 victory there, a stretch of almost a month. "My head has not really been on the ice," said Sekeras. "I need to get my head on the ice." I assumed he was speaking of keeping his focus, his concentration, on the ice. Although with Lubo, you can't be quite certain.

One day after a short game-day practice, Marian Gaborik and Sekeras stayed late to take turns coming in on breakaways, with Manny Fernandez in the net. It was fun to watch the super-quick Gaborik take it in on the equally athletic Fernandez. Sekeras, while not as gifted with the stick, also slipped a puck or two past Manny, and had a habit of yelling "goal" after each of his attempts, whether he scored or not.

The Slovakian sounds reverberated in the empty Xcel Energy Center, and the scene was indeed comical as Sekeras pranced his victory dance around the boards on his way back out to center ice for another try. This was not at all acceptable to Manny, who had been screaming "no goal, no goal" after the failed efforts that Lubomir was celebrating; finally, he burst out of the net on Lubo's final attempt and flat-out tackled him. Gaborik, who saw the move by Fernandez, swooped in to grab the puck and was also tackled by Manny. A scrum ensued, with the three big-league hockey players looking for all the world like the mightiest of mites. It was hilarious, and only ended when a muffled "no goal" was heard from someone at the bottom of the pile, presumably Fernandez. It was one of the best 'boys will be boys' moments I had witnessed during the season.

Marian and Lubomir were a team for the streets as well as the ice. They both hail from Trencin, Slovakia and are pretty good friends, judging from the amount of time they hang out together. Sekeras looked at times like an older brother to Gaborik, and though it was no doubt a good thing to have a fellow countryman for the young star (and top draft pick) to talk with, it was not accomplished fully by design, according to Risebrough.

"It worked out well for us, and there's a little bit of luck involved," said Risebrough. "The other player we considered taking with the Sekeras pick, the younger player, was also a Slovakian. We had thought that it would be nice to have someone that Marian could relate to, but we couldn't know that it would work out as well as it did. I think it's been a big positive for him."

Cam Stewart was more concise in referring to the Gaborik-Sekeras friendship: "I think it made Marian's year," said Stewart, at the end of the season.

"They are friends, and they're both very proud people," said Risebrough. "Both are proud of where they come from, of their country and their city, and they have built on that. They like each other, which is great, and you've got to remember that not all Europeans like each other, just like not all Americans like each other, or all Canadians like each other."

The Europeans are encouraged to have friends and family visit from abroad at different times to keep them company, and to give the guys some different people to share with. During a summer trip to Europe in 2001, Risebrough drove down to Trencin, Slovakia to visit with Lubo and Marian in their home country, visit their home town, and have dinner with their families. "They wanted to show me where they are from. That's how proud they are," says Risebrough. "That's how excited they are to be from Trencin. So these guys are pretty secure in their identities, and it was a great experience."

Doug Risebrough feels it's important for players who come from Europe to the NHL to be committed to their success on this continent. He states a policy to new-comers that, essentially, sets forth that if you come to the Minnesota Wild, you have to stay for the duration. "You can't come with one foot on each continent," says Risebrough. "It's tougher here, simply because this is the NHL."

A lot of players come over and, while they may have been big stars back home, they're more a small piece of a larger puzzle in the NHL. The challenge of accepting a role on the Wild, along with some cultural difficulties, proved too much for the Wild's tough little Russian, Maxim Sushinsky.

Max, who was listed at 5' 10" (but that had to be on his tip-toes), had an ability to stay on the puck and had a good nose for the net. Early in the inaugural season Sushinsky, number 20, proved himself to be a solid performer on offense with back-to-back two-goal games against Edmonton (a 5-3 loss on the road October 15) and Tampa Bay (the Wild's first ever victory, a 6-5 win October 18 at the Xcel Energy Center). The two scores against Tampa came on the power-play, and Max was starting to get a reputation as a finisher who stays with the play and utilizes good positioning around the net.

No one doubts that the Russian had great vision on the ice. But there were questions regarding his ability to get back on defense, and the hot-cold nature of his game. After the Tampa game, Max went a month without scoring, and then had another two-goal game in the 6-1 rout of Boston. One of those goals was on the power-play, and the Wild didn't want to lose the 5th round entry draft selection with the dynamic hands and feet, but there was a little bit of a sense he was slipping away.

Questions about his defense were starting to cut into his playing time, and the challenges of adjusting to life in a foreign country where you don't speak the language (even a little bit) became too much for Max and his family. In several attempted conversations with "Sushi" at the rink, the most English I ever heard him speak was "bad game" after the Chicago Blackhawks loss at home in late October. It was also the *only* English I ever heard him speak. Sushi usually had a smile for me when he saw me in the locker room, but when he was gone in January, it somehow wasn't a complete surprise.

Risebrough was stoic in reference to the Sushinsky endeavor. "We didn't have a great experience with Sushinsky, certainly, but I don't think that it's going to be an inhibitor in the future," he said. "What I think is difficult for some guys to prepare for is how professional it is over here, how intense playing the game is in the NHL. Also, there is a lot more competition for jobs here."

In Russia, Max was part of a select group of people on his team, and the top players can pretty much "ride the wave" with the same bunch of guys all year. If there is movement of players on a team, it usually comes from younger players who are trying to replace the older ones. You don't ordinarily have players being traded out of the team and you don't have players being traded into the team. In the NHL a lot of things can happen during the season. Add to that a more intense travel schedule and more responsibility, and you have a very different hockey environment.

A player like Max was a big star with Avangard Omsk in Russia, his team for the 1999-2000 season. All of a sudden he's struggling a little bit, and the adjustment to life in the NHL toughens. "Sometimes what happens is a player will struggle with the lack of playing time, because he's been a key guy where he comes from and now he's a role player here," stated the Wild GM. "If they can't make some adjustments, if things don't go well right away, they want to go home. I told Max, as I told all of the Europeans, that I wasn't going to send him home in the middle of the season; he was going to be around for the year."

Risebrough winces and then forces a smile as he continues. Sushinsky's agent would refer to Max as "The Russian Gretzky," which he turned out not to be. But Doug is a man with a heart and he let his heart speak a little bit in his dealings with the Sushi-man. "I didn't keep Max here for a couple of reasons; one, I felt he wasn't really fitting in well with the team and, two, I saw a family issue (his wife *really* wanted to go back to Russia) that was perhaps going to be bigger then the hockey point that I was going to make by keeping him here," said Risebrough. "I could have sent him to the minors, to Cleveland, but I chose not to."

"I think I may be paying a little for that now, with some of the players thinking, 'Well, I can go home if I need to.' But I think Max is going to be the last guy to go home under those conditions."

I can still see Max, who was 26 years old while with the Wild, flashing a grin after his two goals in the enormous win over Tampa Bay to put the Wild in the win column for the first time ever. His was a genuine joy that night, and he put a lot of joy in the hearts of Wild fans with his big performance on the St. Paul stage that fall evening. But, ultimately, Max and his wife felt like walleye out of water, and they felt an over-powering need to return to their home.

After a meeting in Risebrough's office, during which his first request to return home was answered with the response that he was under contract and must stay, Max

"Sushi" talks with Stacy Roest.

left the office but returned soon. "I go home," Max pleaded with Risebrough. Doug decided to grant his wish, and Sushinsky was but a memory.

Good luck, Sushi. Thanks for a few great memories.

SEVEN

TOUGH GUYS AND HEAVYWEIGHTS

Hockey's tough guys do some very stupid things on occasion.

Toronto's Tie Domi made an extraordinarily dumb play when he laid out Scott Niedermayer with a flagrant elbow to the head at the end of a Maple Leafs victory in game five of the playoffs against the New Jersey Devils. What was the point of Domi's late game cheap shot? Of course, no explanation is satisfactory, no apology is good enough. Domi says he feels terrible, and he should. If Toronto makes it to a Stanley Cup final in the next few years, he may earn forgiveness.

Until then, Toronto fans can't help but remember the one that got away; a 3-2 lead in the series over the defending Stanley Cup champions, a potentially decisive game six in Toronto and, perhaps most importantly, a red-hot Curtis Joseph in the nets for the Maple Leafs. New Jersey was on its heels. And then disaster, in the form of a cheap shot taken with 12 seconds left, apparently initiated out of meaningless spite in a crucial hockey game. A sleeping giant was awakened in the form of a revitalized New Jersey squad. Playoff hockey is a game of emotion, of momentum and of intensity. Could a mean-spirited gesture gone awry have changed the course of hockey destiny? We'll never know.

There is clearly a difference between genuine toughness and the kind of phony machismo that sometimes passes for toughness in the NHL, but is sometimes a sign of a player's insecurity. Doug Risebrough is looking for men who can bring "true grit" to the Minnesota Wild. He seeks that toughness on the ice, and he knows the difference between players who are genuinely tough and guys who work hard at bluffing their way through.

One player he has respect for is Peter Forsberg, the fine Colorado Avalanche center. Toward the end of the Colorado game that finished the Wild's season, Darby Hendrickson tangled with Forsberg along the boards and even exchanged a few quick blows with the Avalanche's Swedish all-star.

"It was a heat-of-the-moment thing; the end of the game was approaching and we needed the puck," said Hendrickson after the game about the short-lived scuffle. "That guy is one of those rare players who can do it all on a sheet of ice, and you've got to respect him. But I've got to stand my ground, too."

Referring to the 27-year-old center regarded by many of his peers as one of the truly elite players in the game, Darby shook his head in appreciation. "He makes the game look easier than it is with his combination of strength and skill. He's not that big of a guy, but he's such a competitor that he can really take over out there. It's a full time job just to hang with him 'cause he's so smart, so instinctual, that he stays ahead of other players. Forsberg can dictate tempo and make the defender work extra hard. He's a very tough player who can elevate his game for the situation."

Knowing that he admires the way Forsberg plays hockey, it was appropriate to ask what provoked the exchange of punches with him near the Avalanche bench. Hendrickson smiled and tried to recall the moment. "It comes with the territory, and I can't remember exactly why we had that battle," he said about the mini-fight with Forsberg. "I respect Peter Forsberg, and when he has the puck it's darned hard to get it away from him. It's part of the game to move him off the puck, and it's never going to be easy with that guy."

For his part, the Swede spoke highly of both Hendrickson and the Minnesota Wild after the 4-2 Avalanche victory. Walking around the locker room dripping wet with a towel around his waist, the battle-scarred Forsberg doesn't mind spending a moment with a writer. He is wiry and tightly muscular in the manner of an athlete, yet somewhat fragile looking. It's hard to imagine him as an NHL superstar who has won Olympic Gold and even graced his country's postage stamp. He walks with a somewhat unnatural-looking gait as he shuffles through the locker room. With the limp and his still-wet beard glistening, along with a slight hunch and a sly grin, he looks like a Swedish gremlin with big shoulders.

Looks can be deceiving. This is a man who is known league-wide as one of the toughest guys on the ice, with a penchant for developing a steely glare that hardens as the intensity level rises. Like Hendrickson, he doesn't really remember the play that led to the altercation. "I think he hacked me down in our end." Peter Forsberg looks up from a cup of the orange Gatorade he's sipping. "Or maybe I hacked him after he took a shot at me around the net. I think that's what happened. No big deal." He flashes a big smile and says with a soft Swedish accent, "That was a pretty tough game and they're a hard-working bunch of guys. Darby is a good player and a good fit for them. He's a hard worker and you can tell the coaching is strong. They'll be okay here."

Forsberg will be okay, too, hopefully. He's been hurt with such frequency, and with such severity, that he talks of having to take some time off from the game to allow his body to truly heal. Tough guys like Forsberg try to cope with adversity, the kind that cost him an appearance in the 2001 Stanley Cup finals. He underwent emergency surgery to have his spleen removed, and was unable to take the ice during the series with New Jersey. It was a great disappointment, softened only by his team's success.

He wants to continue to play, but is currently facing a reality check with his body. Forsberg missed 33 games during the 1999-00 regular season due to injury. Those absences resulted from this litany of pain: He started the season still rehabilitating his shoulder following offseason surgery, then missed games with a hip pointer in November (two games), suffered a concussion against Vancouver that cost five games, followed by a bruised shoulder (two games) and a separated shoulder (remarkably, only one game missed). And he still had a tremendous playoff run in 2000, a run that was ended in the Western Conference finals by the Dallas Stars in seven games.

When asked about the Wild's tight-checking style of play, the high-flying Swede gave a wince as he responded. "They play it very tight, and it's not my favorite way of playing hockey, let's face it. I like things more open. But if that's what they think they need to do, I can understand that. It's been effective for them."

Forsberg is a speed player with strength who can do it all on the ice, and that includes taking on the heavyweights every now and then. There's the story of how Forsberg knocked Dallas heavy hitter Derian Hatcher to the ice with a mid-ice check while conceding about 50 pounds to the big guy—and then did it again in the exact same place five minutes later, driving Hatcher down with another frontal assault. Tough, strong, resilient, a scorer with grit to spare. That's the way Peter Forsberg is seen by his competitors as well as his teammates.

Interestingly, Wild scout Glen Sonmor likes Derian Hatcher for his rough and tough style of play. A big defenseman who played for the North Stars before the move to Dallas, Hatcher stood tall in the post-game locker room after the Stars' 6-0 drubbing by the Wild. Hatcher faced the tough questions well, leaning back against his road locker, a team captain under siege from a visiting media horde who were still trying to understand what they had just witnessed. When the last ink-stained journalist was gone, he leaned back into his locker and looked around the room, finally moving off for a piece of pizza and a hot shower. He had shown a lot of class with his patience, and Glen Sonmor said he wasn't surprised.

"When I first saw Derian Hatcher years ago, even before he played for the North Stars, he looked somewhat clumsy on the ice, always a little off-balance in relation to the play," said Sonmor. "He's turned out to be a great player, a class act who's probably one of the top ten defenseman in the game. He'll throw in a little offense and he's got a nasty streak that keeps people aware. You gotta like that in a leader." Hatcher plays a smart brand of hockey now. North Star fans may remember him as a fighter who took a lot of penalties, but during the Stars' Stanley Cup run of 1999-00 he totaled only 68 regular season minutes in the penalty box.

The Minnesota Wild faced various tough guys every night they were on the ice during their inaugural National Hockey League season. Bobby Holik, a powerful force for disruption on the New Jersey Devils hockey club, is always getting in the way and messing things up for the opposition. He's a big man playing the center position, 6 feet 4 inches and 230 pounds of physical force who's not afraid to throw his body around, and he takes special pleasure in going after the other team's top player.

"I'm a guy who looks to make as much contact as I can over the course of a game," Holik said in January after the Devils defeated the Wild 4-2 at the Xcel Energy Center. Holik makes his presence on the ice known—if not feared—without drawing an extraordinary number of penalties, finishing fifth on the Devils in time off the ice during the regular season. "That's what I need to do if I'm playing right," said Holik after the game. "Playing hard and using my tools in the right way to win hockey games is what I get paid to do."

Holik must have been playing right when, against the Pittsburgh Penguins in the Eastern Conference finals, he muscled Darius Kasparaitis over the boards and into the New Jersey Devils' bench with a clean check. Then he tried to do the same to Kevin Stevens and almost succeeded, a forceful display of both timing and strength. Holik does this against guys you can't intimidate, but who you can perhaps agitate into making stupid mistakes. Stevens took a retaliation penalty near center ice and, from the penalty box, witnessed a New Jersey score. Mission accomplished, as the Devils went on to win the hockey game 3-1.

A frustrated Kevin Stevens had some choice words to say following that defeat; "When they have to start protecting Bobby Holik in the middle of the ice, we all ought to get out of this thing." Ah, the misery of being out-executed at your own game.

Holik can play some offense as well, with double-digit point totals in the postseason. But it's the constant banging away at the opposition that earns him league-wide respect.

One of the keys to keeping the focus on hockey is to not let the agitators succeed at agitating. The best players know that you've got to keep your composure and focus on the game despite the whacking and hacking that are intended to be a distraction.

It always seems that the guy who retaliates is the player who is certain to end up in the penalty box, not the instigator. One guy the other teams should watch out for in that regard is Wild left wing Cam Stewart, who likes to fly around the ice and mix it up whenever possible. Watch for number 21 when he's on the ice—and when he comes off; he looks almost apologetic when he finishes a shift and has failed to drill somebody. He doesn't take too many unnecessary penalties himself, although he's been known to draw a bunch from irritated opponents. For all the aggravation he causes the players on the other team, the man they call "Stewy" spent a grand total of 18 minutes in the penalty box over 54 games.

He would have liked to play football at the University of Michigan, maybe as a safety. Stewart had the passion for the game, but was perhaps a little on the light side for Big Ten ball. Stewy was a pretty fair high-school linebacker growing up, and he loved a number of different sports as a boy. He played football, lacrosse, soccer and, of course, hockey. When it came time to make a decision regarding a possible future in sports, he decided to play college hockey and went to Michigan for the education as well as the college game.

Stewart's not a big guy, but he makes an effort to leave it all out on the ice every game. At 5' 11" and 195 pounds before toweling off, he's fought the tough battle to stick in the National Hockey League. Early in his career with the Boston Bruins, it seemed every time he got a little comfortable at the major league level, he would find himself back with Providence, Rhode Island of the AHL. The Bruins seemed to like his game when he first arrived after his stint with the Wolverines (he was Boston's 3rd-round draft pick in the '90 entry draft), but not enough to keep him around on a full-time basis.

Stewart was playing in the NHL during his first season as a professional hockey player, skating in 57 games as a rookie with the Bruins. "I was pretty young when I first came to the NHL and maybe I wasn't quite ready. On this team (the Wild), I know my role and feel like I'm making a contribution. This is a blue-collar team without the big stars, and that makes it all the more important to play hard every night and bring my best all the time, every game."

"Cam is one of those guys who's a gamer," said Darby Hendrickson about his teammate. Indeed, it seems that Stewart is one player who never tires of doing the grunt work that is required of him, and he relishes the chance to go head-to-head with the opposition and establish his value to the team. "There are a bunch of guys down in

the minors who can play the game pretty well, and they may never get a shot to play up here. When I was with Houston (of the AHL, where he played the 1997-98 and 1998-99 seasons and scored 36 goals the second year), we had a lot of good players, most of whom aren't up here. I'm going to do anything it takes to stay in the NHL."

Defeating Boston 6-1 had to bring some joy to the sturdy wingman, as did the feeling that the Wild could compete with any team, any time, even on the road. "It's fun for us knowing other teams are respecting us when we come into their buildings. It's a tribute for the whole organization, from the GM to the players," said Stewart.

Stewart has a healthy perspective on what the inaugural season has meant to him, personally. "It's

**Minnesota Wild tough guy
and first Captain Sean O'Donnell.**

been the most fun I've ever had in professional hockey. Some day I'll tell the kids about being a part of the first season of the Minnesota Wild. It's been a blast."

A couple of writers were checking out Scott Parker of the Avalanche after the season finale. He's a big tank of a man, with barbed-wire tattoos and an attitude to go with them. Riding the exercise bike after the game he grunts a "hello" and keeps cranking on the bike, head down, with sweat dripping off his face onto the carpeted floor. This looks like a guy who could get in the ring with Mike Tyson. "There are some guys who can punish you," Glen Sonmor says when asked about Parker. "Some guys look for the tie, for the draw, when they're mixing it up. Parker's not one of them."

Neither is Matt Johnson, the Wild's big left wing. At 6' 5" and 235 pounds, Johnson's a legitimate heavyweight, and he won a few "bouts" this year. In a late season game with Vancouver, he knocked the Canuck's Donald Brashear every which way but loose before their bout ended. First Johnson pummeled Brashear a few times, eventually knocking him to the ice. Then he picked him up and for all the world looked like he was going to send Brashear to the outer limits. But Brashear wasn't moving and, after a pause, Moose set him back down on the ice without delivering a blow. It showed class from the big guy.

Matt Johnson is called "Moose" by those who know and love the tough style of play he embodies. He's plenty big for a left wing and just right for mixing it up with the opposition's toughest characters. That's his job, to enforce the unwritten code of conduct on the ice, which frequently requires him to make sure none of his buddies on the Wild take unnecessary punishment from the other team's rough guys.

Moose might be the toughest son of a gun the Wild has on the roster. Growing up, he was a fan of players like Marty McSorley and Derian Hatcher, and even though he says he respected the talents of a Wayne Gretzky or a Mario Lemieux, he simply liked the guys with steel in their veins a little bit more. "I like to play a physical brand of hockey that is not so much about finesse as it is a willingness to do what's necessary," says Johnson. "That's what playing with toughness is about for me. I'd like to think that I'm a strong forechecker, and I'm willing to drive through people when I have to."

Johnson's not going to score a lot of goals for you, but his duties as a rugged and reliable role player have contributed mightily to some good things happening for his squad, and some disruptive things happening to the other team. His brawl with Donald Brashear during the Wild's 4-3 overtime win in early March was inspirational to the team and a real eye-opener to those who saw the fight. Moose was dominant against one of his fellow heavyweights, and probably won some fans by setting down the wounded Brashear rather than hurting him further.

Matt grew up in California and hung around the beach some during his school days, playing beach volleyball and living well. Somehow it's hard to picture one of the toughest guys in the NHL playing volleyball in the sand, but he enjoyed it and thinks it probably helped him develop as an athlete. This is a man who had to bust his butt to work his way out of the minor leagues, and he's enjoying every minute of the major league ride.

One thing that stands out about Johnson is that he is completely dedicated to doing whatever it takes to help the Wild win hockey games. He's a competitor who responds to the crowd, and credits the fans with inspiring him to not only play tough, but to take on the role of heavyweight fighter when need be. "It's easy to get motivated with the great fans we have in our building. Minnesota is a great place for hockey, and I've been proud to be a member of this team."

Another Wild tough guy during the first season was Sylvain Blouin, who thinks he's a heavyweight even though he's got a light-heavy body. Sylvain Blouin has played a lot of hockey around North America, to say the least. His hockey career has seen him play in the Quebec Major

Andy Sutton lands thunder.

Junior Hockey League, the East Coast Hockey League, the International Hockey League and the American Hockey League. Finally he found an opportunity in the NHL at the age of 26, after spending last season with Worcester of the AHL. It's always good to see Sylvain around the locker room. He has a nice style around people, greeting a visitor with a smile and a friendly hello.

"Sylvy" was a big fan of the Quebec Nordiques as a young man, despite growing up in Montreal. He admired the play of Peter Stastny, a Czech centerman who scored 450 goals in a distinguished NHL career. The youthful Blouin wasn't that kind of offensive force, however, and he caught a big break while playing for Laval of the QMJHL for three years. The Laval team was coached by Bob Hartley, now the leader of the Colorado Avalanche and acknowledged to be one of the best coaches in the NHL. Hartley is considered to be especially effective as a teacher with young players, and he told Blouin what he needed to do to play at the major league level. Sylvy credits Hartley with helping him to improve both his skating and checking, as well as improving the mental toughness that he possesses today.

Blouin has a reputation for being fearless, and he won't back down from anyone on the ice. He did a lot of fighting in the Juniors ("maybe 20 or 25 fights a year"), and that helped to further develop his combative style. He's a tough guy and a heavyweight, in that light-heavy body. Well, kind of a light-heavy body. Seeing him in the locker room, he looks bigger than the 6' 2", 207 pounds at which he's listed in the program. Not taller; broader and thicker. He's a very strong, tough-looking French Canadian along the order of the classic lumberjack type. "I'm not the biggest guy, but I know how to get in there and mix it up. I have a lot of fun on the ice, but I won't take any crap."

Blouin still references his Quebec mentor as "Coach Hartley," giving him the respect of a student who knows the difference he made in his game. "He's certainly proven to be a great coach, so you know that a young player like myself was going to benefit from being around him. It was a great experience playing for him."

The sturdy left wing had an amazing run of offensive play in mid-February, scoring a big goal against Steve Shields and San Jose in a 3-1 win at the Xcel Energy Center on February 18. Blouin's goal helped seal things up against the Sharks, though Scott Pellerin was credited with the game winner. Three days later, against Eddie Belfour, he tallied again in a 6-2 loss at Dallas. Two days after that, he scored the lone Wild goal against Patrick Roy in a 4-1 loss to the Avalanche. Incredibly, Sylvy had scored the first, second and third NHL goals of his career, his only goals of the season, in back-to-back-to-back games against three of the top goalies in the League. He was kind of floating around the locker room for a couple of days after his goal scoring spree.

How do you explain all that offense, Blouin was asked one day? Blouin is one of the top enforcers on the Wild, but his three-goal spurt, along with his brawn, may have helped secure his future in the NHL. "It's hard to put a finger on it, exactly," said Blouin, whose offensive production will always be a bonus for the Wild. "It took a while to get the first one, and then it kind of flowed. To score against Patrick Roy, who I grew up watching on TV when he played for Montreal, was kind of like a dream. Hard work can pay off, and there's some of the proof."

If Blouin is a light-heavyweight, Wild defenseman Andy Sutton is a kind of super-heavyweight. He's a really big hockey player, and at 6' 6" and 250 pounds, he looks like he could play defensive end in the NFL. He has a look about him that's "GQ" when he is attired in his good duds, but he's a tough guy on the ice. There are those who wish he would play a little tougher. "I'd like to see him be a little more of a bully," said one NHL scout. "He could be more of a tough guy than he is."

Sutton wasn't happy in San Jose, and he was pleased when the Wild acquired him. He felt the coaching staff did not treat him well in California, saying "they weren't very up front about what they expected from me, and things just kind of deteriorated from there." It was Andy who was involved in the first-ever fight at the Xcel Energy Center when he tangled with the Philadelphia Flyers winger Gino Odjick during the first period of the home opener. He headed off the ice at 13:57, "credited" with the Wild's first major penalty, in a bout that was pretty much a win for Sutton. Odjick, who finished the season with Montreal, is a tough guy, but he was giving away three inches and about 35 pounds to Sutton.

Sutton played right wing in a November game against the New York Rangers, and enjoyed the opportunity to display a little more of his offensive game. He was a winger in college at Michigan Tech until Pierre Page (with an assist from Glen Sonmor) suggested to his college coach that Andy might be better suited on the blue line. "I enjoy the physical side of the game, and while I'm not the fastest guy on the ice, if I can catch somebody coming across the middle and hit them clean, I'm fast enough," Sutton said.

I had been told by a friend in the hockey business to be ready for Larry Hendrickson, Darby's dad. "He's a bit of a wild character," the hockey man had said. Darby told me later that he thinks his dad's reputation may be a bit overstated, though. "I think he's a great coach, as I've often said. He has a lot of depth." Larry won a phenomenally exciting state championship coaching at the high school level in 1997 when his Apple Valley team defeated Duluth East in the semifinals in *five overtimes,* and went on to defeat Edina in the final.

He has a lot of tough guy in him, as well. At 5 feet 10 inches and 215 pounds, he's not as solid as he was when he played all-state quality football for Washburn High in Minneapolis. He was pointed more towards football, though his first love was hockey. Larry had bench-pressed 305 pounds prior to one of our conversations, and he was justifiably proud of it. "Not too bad for a guy who's 58 years old," he said.

Not too bad, indeed. There are a lot of players in the NHL who'd like to be able to bench press 300 pounds. He does have a little bit of the wild man in him, though. When Darius Kasparaitis, the Lithuanian tough guy for the Penguins took a cheap shot at Darby and knocked him out of that game and a few more with a concussion, the old man was riled. But Larry was only kidding when he told me he was looking for flights to Europe to go find Kaspo's father. At least I think he was kidding.

"I think I should go find his old man and kick his butt. What's the deal with that number? Kasparaitis throws a lot of cheap shots and everybody knows it," Larry said. "He's coming at guys from behind and dishing out crap all the time. I'm serious. I'd like to have a minute or two with his old man. We could straighten things out."

Larry has a few ideas regarding knocking out the cheap stuff that keeps popping up in the game. Injuries like the one suffered by Darby at the hands of Kasparaitis result in the loss of a key player for the injured party's team, while the offender usually serves a couple minutes and moves on with his hockey life. That doesn't seems right.

"My thought is that if you hurt a guy enough to knock him out of action *and take a penalty,* then the offender comes back when the player comes back," says Larry.

Doesn't sound like a bad idea. Kasparaitis would have gone to the penalty box and perhaps completed the game. After the game, a review of the incident would be made by league officials. When a determination of accuracy is made, that would be the trigger for some kind of parallel suspension procedure. That should cut down on some of the slashing and hacking, as well as the kind of wild elbow Tie Domi threw to injure Scott Niedermayer in the Stanley Cup playoffs. Most players are not stupid; they want to get away with fouls and stay on the ice. The league needs to make the penalties tougher for serious infractions, something more than the occasional after-the-fact suspension and small fine.

So, what is a true hockey tough guy in the mind of Larry Hendrickson? It's not the violence and it's not the phony stuff. It's going into the corner first and getting into the scrap without fear. It's taking the hit to keep the puck in. "I like the way Matt Johnson goes in there and pounds, and Wes Walz is tough and aggressive. Aaron Gavey and Antti Laaksonen are strong, along with Cam Stewart and a few others. There's a bunch of tough guys on the Minnesota Wild. You better be tough to play for Jacques Lemaire.

"The point is that real tough guys play hard and don't count on the other guy to make the play. One thing I've learned from watching a lot of hockey is the genuinely tough people in the game aren't afraid to try and get it done, no matter what. They take responsibility."

Darby Hendrickson saw another side to Tie Domi, having played with Domi in Toronto for the better part of two years. He has good memories of the rough-and-tumble right wing, as well as of Domi's fellow enforcer, left wing Kris King. Darby was the center on a line that featured the tough guys on either side, and while the group had some success offensively, they didn't do as well as they would have liked.

"Kris King was a hard-working, honest guy who was a decent left-handed shooter. He was a 'Captain' type of guy, vocal in the locker room and a good team player. Not necessarily the most talented guy, which I think he would admit, but a guy who worked hard every day and loves the game," recalled Darby. "Then you have Tie Domi on the right wing, who is one of the toughest guys in the whole league. Tie has a lot of confidence in himself, and he can get things done on the ice. I know that he has really improved his game. He was strictly a fighter when he came into the league, but like I say, he's a great skater and much improved.

"We used to locker pretty close to each other. Before one game, Kris was taping his stick and saying to me, 'Darby, don't pass me the hockey puck. Don't pass it to the left side, you know I'm not a very good hockey player.' He was laughing, but maybe serious in a way, too.

"A few moments later, Tie Domi's on the other side of me, and I don't think he heard Kris talking. He starts saying, 'Hey, Darby, get me the puck! I want the puck. You carry it up and get it to me; get me the puck! You've got to set me up!' That's how different their personalities were.

"You know, we had a lot of fun playing together. They were great guys. If anybody went after me, those guys would annihilate 'em. And sometimes we would really dominate down low, forechecking our butts off and getting good opportunities. We didn't put enough pucks in the net, though, bottom line. We didn't have as much goal scoring success as we wanted."

Darby stands by the fact that Domi is a good guy, despite the Niedermayer incident in game six in Toronto, and notes that Domi is a very popular player among Maple Leaf fans. "He does a lot of charity work that the public never hears about. I'll tell you this about Tie; he will never let down a teammate who needs support, he will always stick up for them. That's a great quality to have as a hockey player."

It's also a quality shared by the Wild's first captain, Sean O'Donnell, who once told me "first job is to look out for my teammates and make sure they know I've got them covered. I'll be there to stand up for them whenever things get rough, no matter what's going on or who's involved. That's what being an 'enforcer' is all about."

It was a tough year for Tie Domi. His first brush with trouble occurred when a fan got out of line and fell into the penalty box in Philadelphia. A man was taunting Domi from outside the box when the glass gave way, with the non-athletic looking fan tumbling into the pit, so to speak, and meeting with somewhat predictable results. Domi lit into the guy a few times (he probably could have killed him) before things were broken up. For this unusual event, which he didn't provoke, the league was not too hard on him.

I can't help but think that Tie Domi must be a decent guy to be held in high regard by Darby Hendrickson. Domi has denied that he was aiming for Neidermayer's head, and says he merely wanted to leave a message with a solid shoulder hit. Most people around the NHL are not buying that excuse. One NHL scout I spoke with says he does not accept the suggestion that Domi had intended to hit Niedermayer in the shoulder, and merely missed his target.

"What Tie Domi did in the game with the Maple Leafs was utter foolishness," the scout said. "Toronto was really going and Curtis Joseph was playing like a man possessed. And then it was all gone. If Tie Domi's going to get a guy, he's not going to nail him in the shoulder, if that's what he said. He's gonna take him out. And that's what he did. At the same time, he's a human being and he's going to make mistakes, but hey, you've got New Jersey on the ropes and you screw up like that? You've got to be crazy."

Anaheim scout Mike McGraw has an intense dislike of "hired guns," whose role on the ice is only to intimidate or possibly injure. "If you're not a hockey player, go out and do something else with your life," he says bluntly. "You shouldn't be out there if you're not a hockey player, it's as simple as that. All the stick swinging and hacking, running around injuring guys, serves no purpose in the game."

So who does Mike McGraw respect for authentic toughness on the ice? "Scott Stevens (of the New Jersey Devils) is an example of a guy who can play hockey and is tough as steel. He doesn't get challenged a lot because he can play the game fundamentally well, and he's not gonna take a lot of crap. During the course of his career, he's proven that he is the real deal. Guys around the league know that you mess with Scott Stevens at your own risk, because he can hurt you in a lot of different ways."

Minnesota Tough Guys: February 26, 1981

There was doubt in the Minnesota North Star locker room that the team was ever going to beat the Boston Bruins. They hadn't won at the Garden in 14 years of trying, and Minnesota coach Glen Sonmor was tired of the licking that his team was taking in the newspapers, from the crowd, and *especially* on the ice.

"Enough was enough," Sonmor remembers. "We would go to Boston and the intimidation factor was always there and it was huge. The media would take shots at us, the other team had no respect for us and I told our guys in a pregame meeting we had to respond that night. I told them we were not going to take any intimidation, and the first time they tried to push us around we were going after 'em. Not the second time, not the third time; the first time they pulled anything, our guys had to stand their ground."

Sonmor's challenge was a dramatic test for his team. He felt he had to break with the negative tradition that had been established over the years. In the late 70's, as the story goes, John Wensink of the Bruins skated over to the North Star bench

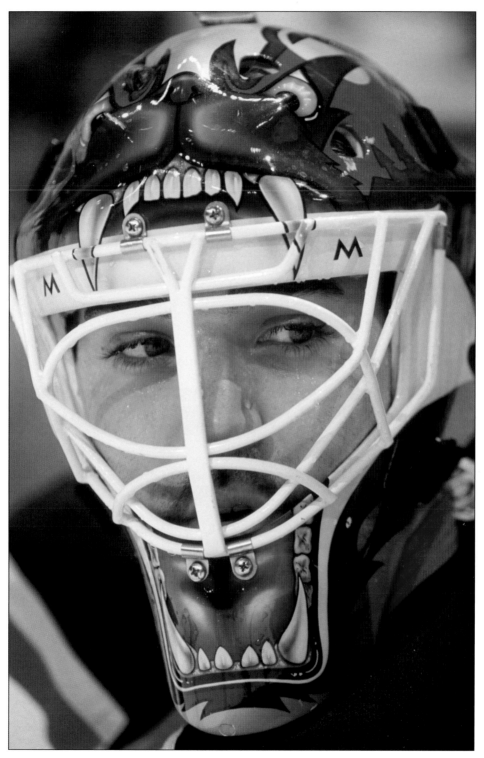

Manny Fernandez readies for combat.

Opening night at the Xcel Energy Center, October 11, 2000.

St. Paul Mayor Norm Coleman with Sean O'Donnell—ceremonial puck drop on opening night.

The 2000–01 Minnesota Wild.

Jaques Lemaire in his element behind the bench.

Darby Hendrickson celebrates a score against Detroit.

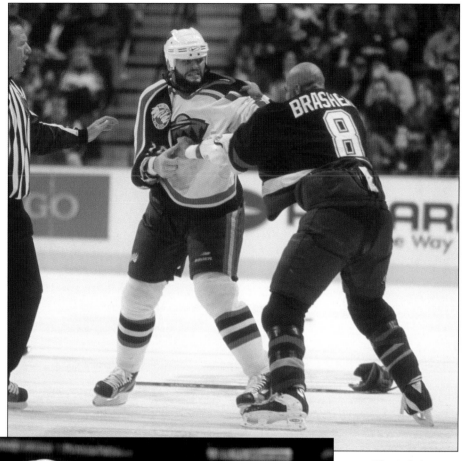

Matt Johnson battles Donald Brashear.

Sean O'Donnell has the jersey up.

Cam Stewart tumbles...

...and Stewart delivers a big blow.

Curtis Leschyshyn, Brad Bombardir, and Scott Pellerin share a Wild moment.

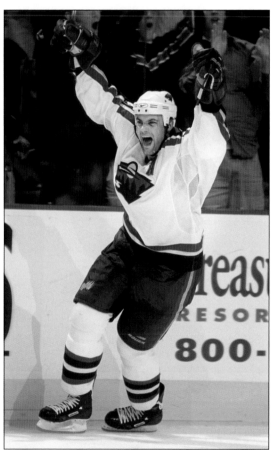

Curtis Leschyshyn rejoices after scoring the game-winning goal vs. Pittsburgh.

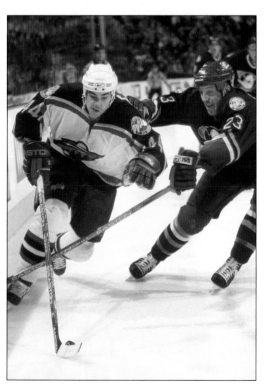

Aaron Gavey on the move.

Sylvain Blouin readies a right hand.

The Czech—Slovak connection.

Jeff Nielsen pushes up the ice.

Antti Laaksonen stuffs one home against the San Jose Sharks.

The fans give a salute.

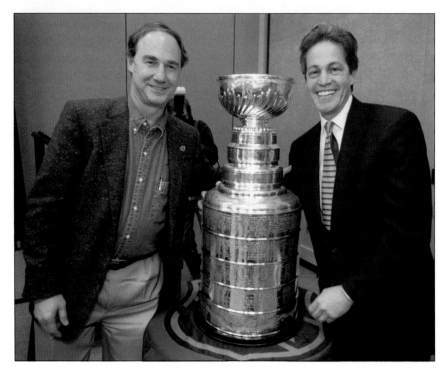

***Wild CEO Jac
Sperling and
Norm Coleman
with the
Stanley Cup.***

An intense Wes Walz readies for a face-off.

One of the fastest players in the game: Wes Walz.

The Wild celebrate the home overtime victory against Detroit.

Wes Walz pots one of his seven short-handed goals.

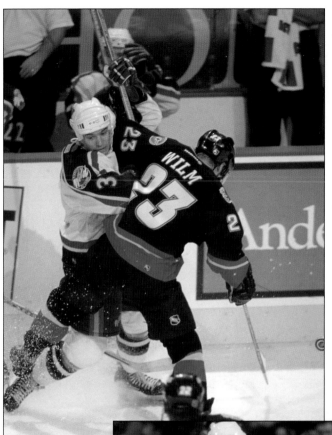

Wild defenseman Ladislav Benysek played tough hockey all year.

Scott Pellerin was the Wild captain for the month of November.

Always a threat: Marian Gaborik moves on the offensive end.

Jamie McLennan—glove save!

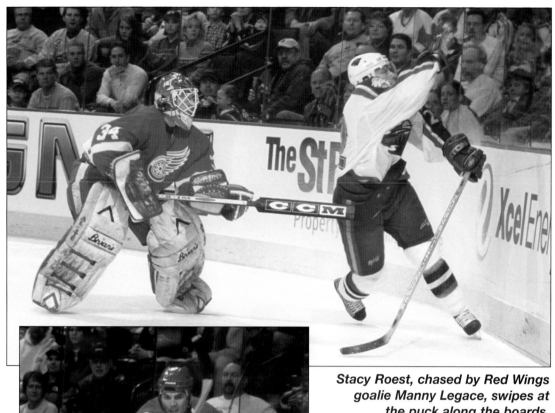

Stacy Roest, chased by Red Wings goalie Manny Legace, swipes at the puck along the boards.

Darby Hendrickson rides 'em high.

Lubomir Sekeras and Manny Fernandez celebrate a win.

Bob Naegele, Jr. visits with the Wild Faithful.

and challenged the entire team to a fight. Nobody budged and the 6-foot, 200-pound Wensink simply skated away, completely unscathed.

"I told the players if we battled right from the start, it wouldn't guarantee that we would win, but that we would never win until we stood up to the Bruins," said Sonmor. "Every time we visited Boston we could read about what a weak bunch we were, and the guys on the other team would talk stuff the whole game. This had been going on since we came into the league. No more."

The puck was dropped for the opening face-off, and when Bruin center Steve Kasper raised his stick into Bobby Smith's groin, the gloves were off within seconds. The rest of the night was a brawl that couldn't be contained, with 406 minutes in penalties assessed on the night, still an NHL record, as is the 211 minutes given to the Minnesota team and the 67 combined penalties in the first period alone.

The North Stars didn't win that night, but they were a different hockey team after the game. "The league had some questions for me about what happened that night. It really got rough out there; at one point I looked out on the ice and there were five fights going on, *and we were winning all of them,*" recalled Sonmor. "There wasn't a guy on our team who didn't stand up.

"It was something like the kid who stands up to the schoolyard bully and takes a few lumps while giving a few back. The boys were proud that they did what they had to do, and the penalties were a part of the deal," remembered Sonmor.

"When we went back out to Boston for the playoffs, we knocked them off in back-to-back games, then beat 'em at home and took the series 3-0 on our way to the Stanley Cup finals!"

EIGHT

WINNERS

After knocking off the Dallas Stars on December 17 by the score of 6-0, the Wild began a furious run of high-quality games. They gained a tie against high-flying Ottawa 2-2 at home (in front of a 20th consecutive sell-out crowd) on fine goaltending by Jamie McLennan (31 saves) and a couple of goals from Darby Hendrickson that brought them back from a 2-0 deficit. They beat L.A. 4-3 a couple of nights later with help from a big game by Sergei Krivokrasov (goal, assist), as the teams combined for an Xcel Energy Center record six goals in the 3rd period.

It was on to Detroit, where the Wild extended their unbeaten streak to four games by scoring four straight goals after the Wings' Sergei Federov scored the game's first two goals in the opening period. "I had Jac Sperling over to my house," recalled Wild President Tod Leiweke. "We were watching it on Fox (TV) and stayed with the game when (the Wild) fell behind. It didn't look good after Federov's goals. When our guys came roaring back, it was tough to contain Jac!" For good reason. It was a huge victory in the first game ever against the proud Red Wings.

There followed a 2-2 tie at home with the Phoenix Coyotes. Jim Dowd scored the goal that tied the game in the 3rd period and was a part of several Wild flurries that barely failed to clinch a victory. The Wild outshot the Coyotes 27-24, including 18-8 in the 2nd and 3rd periods. The Wild extended their unbeaten streak to six games by defeating the Anaheim Mighty Ducks 3-2 at the Xcel Energy Center. The boys from Disney pressed Manny Fernandez to the finish, outshooting the Wild 31-26, but Manny was stellar and made some big saves near the end. After a 1-1 tie with Atlanta, extending the unbeaten run to seven games, the stage was set for a rematch with Detroit.

The Minnesota Wild were now undefeated in their past seven games entering the Friday evening contest against the Detroit Red Wings at the Xcel Energy Center in early January. The Red Wings were already a part of the unbeaten streak following the 5-3 Wild victory at Joe Louis Arena a couple of days after Christmas. That game had been widely reported in the media as being of great embarrassment to the tradition-rich Detroit franchise, and why shouldn't it have been?

The Red Wings are loaded with talented players ranging from future Hall of Famers to perennial all-stars to the merely solid. Most of them are a part of the group that won Stanley Cups in 1997 and 1998, and they have a coach, Scotty Bowman, who has won eight Stanley Cups (which ties him with the legendary Toe Blake for the most Cup championships ever) and more games than anyone else in history. But there was more to be considered about the Red Wings' situation during the 2000-01 season.

Detroit is a franchise that is getting a little long in the tooth. A number of the team's best players are over 30, including guys like Brendan Shanahan and Sergei Fedorov. Meanwhile, Steve Yzerman, Chris Chelios, Larry Murphy, Steve Duchesne, Igor Larionov, Doug Brown and Pat Verbeek are all over 35 years old. Their number one goaltender, Chris Osgood, had been playing so poorly that he had been pushed aside by long time minor-leaguer Manny Legace. Steve Yzerman had missed over 20 games with a knee injury, and Chris Chelios would be out until at least March following knee surgery. Darren McCarty, Kris Draper, and Brent Gilchrist hadn't played as expected. Key players, for one reason or another, were not giving the team what they had in the past.

That said, you have to give the Wild a lot of the credit for the earlier 5-3 win. Detroit's aging veterans tend to turn it up when they need to, and that's a dangerous way to play against a hustling team like the Wild. The Minnesotans have young legs and they played with fire to beat Detroit on the road, despite being outshot 37-23. Manny Fernandez made a number of difficult stops among his 34 saves and was strong throughout. "We played one of our best games," said Jim Dowd, who garnered two assists in the contest. "Our aggressive play in the offensive end when we had a few chances gave us a lead, and Manny wouldn't give it up."

If the Red Wings were looking to recover their top form, they had to believe that a rematch with the Wild would give them a continued boost. They were playing improved hockey now, with victories over St. Louis and Colorado in the days leading up to the second game against Minnesota. Jacques Lemaire was ready for the challenge, but also thought his team was capable of playing better than they had during the recent undefeated streak. "I do feel we've played better hockey at other times this season," said the Wild coach, perhaps remembering the 36 shots that had resulted in just one goal against Atlanta two nights earlier. "We need to finish the good plays that we make. Our goalies are playing well and that's been the key for us. Detroit is one of the very good teams in the league and we'll see how we do this time."

Jacques was right. The goaltending had been exceptional during the Wild's current run, with Jamie McLennan playing very well in ties against Ottawa, Phoenix and Atlanta, and Manny Fernandez undefeated in his last six starts. It would be Fernandez, who'd played so well in the first game between the two teams, in the net against Detroit in the rematch.

Lemaire said he was concerned about the Wild staying with the Red Wings from the outset. "Detroit had a big game last night (with Colorado) and they'll be fired up from the start," he told a journalist a couple of hours before faceoff. "We'll have to be ready."

The Wild were indeed ready for the task from the moment the puck was dropped, with Jeff Nielsen scoring on Minnesota's first shot of the game just 26 seconds into the action. After taking a tip pass from Antti Laaksonen at the blue line, he skated past defenseman Kirk Maltby and put a backhand under goalie Chris Osgood. Detroit tied the score at 1-1 on their first shot of the game when Darren McCarty took a feed from Steve Yzerman to beat Fernandez shorthanded at 3:18, while Igor Larionov was off the ice serving a double-minor for high sticking.

Filip Kuba put the Wild ahead 2-1 while scoring his first power play goal during a two-man advantage. Sekeras fired a nice pass to Scott Pellerin, whose touch pass hit Kuba on the stick. Filip's powerful wrist shot beat Osgood to the glove side. It was a solid stretch of offensive play for the Wild, with Andy Sutton moving guys around while playing forward.

"I thought Andy helped us out on that goal," said Pellerin after the game. "He was really working and opened up a few lanes. Detroit is so good at bottling things up and preventing the kind of movement you want."

The Wild had outshot Detroit 14-7 in the first period, but were outshot 10-8 in the second. During the third period, Fernandez was trying to withstand a steady barrage of shots by Detroit players, who put 17 on net during the session. But the Red Wings' only goal came on a power play opportunity by Pat Verbeek at 3:36, and it was on to overtime.

It was Kuba who saved the Wild from another tie by scoring the game-winner at 2:58. The Wild had come out flying in the extra period and were able to keep the puck under their control. Detroit had no shots in overtime when Stacy Roest fed a pass to Kuba, who wound up and essentially fanned on the shot. The puck was dumped to the corner, where Detroit seemed to focus all its attention. Roest was in there battling and ended up with the puck, firing it again to Kuba who snapped a quick sliding shot that never left the ice past Osgood.

There was absolute bedlam at the Xcel Energy Center as the Wild had defeated the Red Wings for a second straight time. Final score; Minnesota Wild 3, Detroit Red Wings 2.

There were a number of heroes in the Minnesota victory, including Nielsen, whose quick score ignited the Wild early in the game. Roest, Wes Walz, and Antti Laaksonen all played solid games. But it was Kuba and Fernandez who were the stars of the game. It was Kuba's first-ever two-goal game in the NHL and the timing couldn't have been better. Fernandez extended his unbeaten streak to seven games, including five consecutive victories.

"When it's time to put the hammer down, we do it," said the goaltender after stopping 32 shots and improving to 12-7-2 on the season. "Going into the third period, it was like a playoff game for us. If we don't make the playoffs, this is going to be the playoffs for us."

Detroit's General Manager, Ken Holland, is sensitive to the fact that, while the Red Wings had a strong record during the regular season, they were really waxed in the playoffs by the Los Angeles Kings. After the Kings fell behind 2-0 in the series by losing the first two games in Detroit, Los Angeles won four straight games to close out the Red Wings. When Los Angeles knocked them out, you knew there would be changes coming.

Holland became very proactive and acquired Brett Hull, who should add some punch to the Red Wings' already strong (if ancient) offensive machine. Dominik Hasek should solidify the goaltending, but "The Dominator" is over 35 himself, as is Hull. Clearly, Detroit is not playing for second place. They want to get to the Stanley Cup finals, and they want to do it now. Scotty Bowman was not expected to return for

2001-02, but he will be behind the bench for one more run. The Red Wings want to get over the hump and win a title before they have to rebuild, and when they rebuild, they'll do it with a new coach.

Doug Risebrough recalled the Detroit overtime contest as a splendid moment in the building of a Wild tradition. "What a classic battle, with the winning goal coming so suddenly," remembered Risebrough. "I can still see Filip Kuba skating over to the boards, with his arms raised and his back to the glass, hands in the air. All the players skated towards him, and the fans were pounding the glass; it was an amazing scene, and Kuba had never had a moment like that in the NHL before.

"Now, if you're a player who's going to join this team, that's what you're going to have to live up to. You have to live up to playing that hard, in this building, for this team. There is a standard that has been set. I think the crowd's reactions to those moments is what has really created the soul of our franchise. This is not going to be a fun place to play if you're the opposition, but it's going to be an inspiring place to play for us.

"The fan's reaction to the players created a number of special moments that people will talk about for years." Risebrough turns serious as he speaks, and reaches for a pen to turn over in his hand. He punctuates his words with light taps on the desk, then pulls the pen back, and it disappears into his big hands. "For me it means that we have set a kind of standard; we can say to all players, including prospective players, 'here's what happened on this given night, in these circumstances, and we're very proud of it.' And I think the fans are proud of what has been established."

It is impressive to see this man, who has won championships at the highest level of hockey on more than one occasion, be moved by what transpired during the Minnesota Wild's first year and by what he believes is yet to come. "I can take no credit for this, but probably the biggest plus that this team had was the fans," said Risebrough. "It was a very inspiring situation for the players all year, as well as for the staff, to walk in and see so much genuine enthusiasm for the team. And it was more than that; it was enthusiasm for the game itself, for hockey, and for the particulars of the game. Everyone had to see this as being something unique.

"There's a soul in this building. There's a consciousness in this building. There's an expectation that you're going to come and see something special when you walk in the door. We had a lot of great moments, and we're fortunate to have these things to build on. Take the Dallas game, as one example. People will talk about that game for 20 years. Here you have the goalie (Fernandez) who was traded from Dallas getting the shutout, you have both Minnesotans scoring goals, you beat the team that left here, and they leave without scoring a goal; the script couldn't have been written any better.

"The story that I like to tell about that game is the way the players reacted to a very intense situation, an intimidating and pressure-packed setting, and they went out there and gave their all. They really gave the fans something to cheer about."

The unbeaten streak was a part of the magic, the proof in the pudding that this was no ordinary expansion franchise. It began with the dismantling of the two-time defending Western Conference champion Dallas Stars, 6-0, and included two victories over the powerful Detroit Red Wings. Yes, there was emotion. And there was pride in the success the team was achieving. But more than that it was team play, the system at its best. It was the "control" Jacques emphasizes, working to magical perfection. Jacques is teaching his Wild men the intricacies of the game, a game that he learned as a player from boyhood through eight Stanley Cup championships. His new team had been surprisingly strong to start the year, but now they were a wonder!

And something else was happening to the Wild players. They had been blessed by opportunity to somehow, through fortune or perceived misfortune, end up playing for a tremendous hockey man determined to give to them all that he has learned, to teach and share the accumulated wisdom of the years. For a number of the players who continued to develop, his magic was taking hold. This humble yet proud man understands the game like few others, he understands what it takes to be outstanding, and he understands people and how to work with them to gain the best of their ability. He takes great pride in watching his charges do the best they can and, win or lose, evaluating them on effort, because that is the most important player growth consideration at this point in the development of the franchise.

Doug Risebrough is the type of manager who depends on his people; he counts on his staff to bring him the best information available. That's what head scouts Tommy Thompson and Guy Lapointe do. You have to trust your people but there were times Risebrough went with his gut instinct and trusted his intuition.

"Wes Walz was the type of find where it took a bit of a leap of faith. He had obviously underperformed, in some people's minds, because he had been out of the league for a few years. I believed he could be a good two-way player. We knew he had speed and I felt he could check if he dedicated himself to it. He adds tempo to the game with his speed and the way he pursues the puck.

"The acquisition of Antti Laaksonen went the same way, on kind of a hunch. Here's a European player who brings speed, can check and will make some plays, but we don't have to rely on him to be a top offensive guy. Kuba is a guy who has some tools; I'd heard a lot about him over the last couple of years, and one of our scouts said to try to get him. (The scout) had been watching Filip play quite a bit, and felt strongly about him. The results with Kuba, so far, have been very good."

Then you have a player like Darby Hendrickson, whose reappearance in Minnesota hockey seemed to work a little like a movie script. First he makes the squad, then he starts playing some good hockey, including scoring the first goal ever at the Xcel Energy Center. He follows that up by playing great in the pounding of the former North Stars, then has a healthy baby boy, Mason, a few weeks later with his wife Dana. To cap everything off, he becomes the Wild captain for the last several weeks of the season and finishes the year as a leading scorer.

Risebrough gets a funny look when asked about the hard-working local hero from Richfield, Minnesota. "Even with all the scouting I had done, I hadn't seen Darby play very much. (Scout) Terry Simpson was on our staff last year, and he was a very strong supporter of Hendrickson. He liked him as a player and as a person; I think he said 'here's what you're going to get...,' so I felt like I had a pretty good read on him.

"Darby was another interesting guy in terms of talking to people around the league. Everyone wanted to see good things happen to Darby, and really stood up for him. There I was at the expansion draft and even the Vancouver people (Darby's previous team) were saying, 'this is a really good guy, you should take him.' Some teams wouldn't want to let a good player go, so they wouldn't tell you that. They saw this as a unique opportunity for Darby.

"We knew we were getting a quality guy, but we didn't know what level he could get to as a player. So, clearly, this was a very inspiring setting for him and Darby achieved a lot."

Lou Vairo is a New Yorker with strong opinions and a lot of character. He works for USA hockey and has coached national teams on several occasions. "I had heard that Darby Hendrickson was a 4th-string major leaguer and didn't think too much of his being on the team. I knew he was a good guy who might fit in when needed.

"Then I got to coach him (on the 2001 National Team) and my thinking changed. When I got to see him play, all previous notions of his quality as a player went out the window. There was a situation where Dave Legwand got hurt and the coaches (Vairo and assistants Mark Johnson and Dean Blaise) decided to stick him out there, and he played tremendous hockey.

"When I talked to Doug Risebrough, I shared my opinion about Darby being a quality guy who I thought could be a strong NHL player. Darby was one of those guys who needed an opportunity to gain confidence and have some success. I saw Doug (Risebrough) later in the year and he told me 'You were right, Lou. He can play.' "

Speaking with Risebrough about a couple of Wild players, I used the word 'tenacity' to describe their play, as in "Walz showed a lot of tenacity in the Vancouver game going into the corners and playing some long, grinding shifts." I was trying to get Doug to talk about what he looks for in a player, and while he agreed with my assessment of Walz's play, he wanted to explore the concept of tenacity in a little more depth.

"That's an interesting word," Risebrough said. "A player needs to be tenacious in that he needs to be optimistic that he's going to overcome some of the hardships that he is going to face, both mental and physical. That's what tenacity is really about at this level. Professional sports involve competition both *external and internal*. There are a lot of battles a National Hockey League player will face, and they are continuous; he needs to fight to win a job and he also needs to fight to keep his job. And then he has the responsibility of trying to defeat the opposition in games.

"My biggest worry is that I'll get a guy who's not enjoying playing the game, who doesn't have the passion for all that it takes to succeed. Those are the personnel mistakes I worry about most. If I find a player who has the passion and the discipline, the rest of it will fall into place. There's a lot of pressure at this level; there's a need to be consistent at all times. The *internal* pressure is pretty much a constant in the NHL. You have to be able to handle that. Passion for the game and a tolerance for adversity are the fundamental keys to being a winner. It's not always the excitable types who give you the most."

Risebrough dug into his hockey past to reference a player he had great respect for and with whom he'd played for a couple of years. Late in his career, Risebrough was a member of Calgary's esteemed "Over the Hill" line with John Tonelli and Lanny McDonald from 1986-88. It was there that he got to know a player by the name of Joey Mullen.

"Joey Mullen wasn't a twitchy, sparky kind of guy," said Risebrough. "He'd be sitting quietly off in the corner half the time, not a live-wire type of person. I don't know if you would describe Joey as tenacious. But when the game was on the line, when it really counted, that's who you wanted out there."

A look at Mullen's numbers in Calgary reveal the type of player Risebrough remembers. During his years with the Flames, from 1985 through 1990, Mullen scored 190 goals and had 198 assists. A total of 388 points in 345 games, with only 95 penalty minutes for the five-year stretch. In 1988-89 he had 51 goals and 59 assists for a total of 110 points. Joe Mullen wasn't one of those guys skating all over the ice banging into the boards for show, but he was a winner, and that's having the right kind of tenacity for Risebrough. He's looking for performance and results, true professionalism in the pursuit of victory.

"Riser"

Herb Brooks almost made the talented Doug Risebrough a Gopher defenseman in the early '70's, before Risebrough decided to stay in Canada and turn professional. He would have been the only Canadian on a team that would go on to capture the national title.

"I was more than 'almost' a Minnesota hockey player. I was all but there! Probably the two things that hurt, that kept it from happening, were that I was a nineteen-year-old at the time, and I had never been drafted by the (junior hockey) Ontario Hockey League. I got picked up by Kitchener, which was 12 miles from where I was living. And my mother had just given birth to my sister, who's the youngest of six siblings, and I really felt that I couldn't pass up the chance to live at home, play at Kitchener and watch my sister grow up for a year and a half. That's what prevented me from becoming a Gopher.

"But I was really impressed when I came down here to be with Herb and saw his vision of what he was working toward. Ultimately that came to be, and you know that for every player who wanted to play on a 'winner,' Herbie was committed to that goal. But the ironic thing was that the same year he won his first national championship, I won my first Stanley Cup with Montreal.

"Herbie told me that I was the only Canadian player he was going to bring in. I thought it was great when he stood up later and announced that he had won the championship with (a team that was) all Americans. Well, at the same time, I was standing up and saying that I had won a Stanley Cup with the Canadiens. I was just 21 years old. It worked out pretty good for both of us."

NINE

THE NEED TO FINISH

A conversation with Jacques Lemaire after the first Nashville contest gave indication of a growing concern about the lack of offensive production on the Wild power play. The Wild lost the game 2-1, their only score coming on a goal from Darby Hendrickson at 5:22 of the opening period. Their opportunities seemed to dwindle as the game went on. The Wild took 12 shots in the first period, eight in the second and six in the third to outshoot the Predators 26-19 for the game, but they couldn't convert several strong chances around the goal, particularly when the Minnesotans had the man advantage.

The goal by Hendrickson, his fourth of the season, assisted by Aaron Gavey and Sergei Krivokrasov, gave Minnesota a strong start that they couldn't build on. Nashville came back to score a pair of goals just three minutes apart in the second period, (the game winner netted by Cliff Ronning on a shot that Jamie McLennan appeared to have a play), and that was it for the scoring. It wasn't the end of good scoring opportunities for the Wild, particularly during some power play chances that went unfulfilled. Jacques Lemaire was looking for some answers to questions that would be asked all season long.

"I have to be thinking about the way we move on the power play," said Lemaire. "We need to have a spark out there; that's what we seem to lack. There's not enough fire when we're a man up. I will ask the guys, 'where's the energy?'"

Jacques stroked his chin as he mulled over the effort his team had just put forth, looking rather contemplative, even by this thoughtful man's standards. He doesn't usually complain about a lack of energy—quite the contrary, that is what he's most proud of his charges for possessing: a great will to play hard and leave it all out on the ice. But the lack of Wild success with the man advantage was becoming noticeable.

"We could use a few more shots on net to help us break out, but it seems like there were times we should have scored. I'm not sure why we're not scoring. The strong forechecking should lead to some rebounds and some goals." Jacques paused and scratched his head, perhaps a little more tired than usual after a game. There was just a hint of frustration with his team's execution.

"I think maybe the guys are spending too much time looking for the perfect shot," he said. "We need to put the puck in the net more than we are doing, that's for sure, and I think we need to keep pressure on, skate hard to the net and shoot the puck. Goals should come," he says in a determined voice. Against Nashville, the goals would never come on the power play—the Wild went 0-19 for the season with the man advantage against the Predators.

One thing the Wild had not been doing very well during their first season was score on the power play, and during the course of the year there had been a few signs of frustration in that area from the coach, though not many. As one NHL scout put it, "the Wild are pretty good at the set-up and the passing, but they have trouble finishing. It's kind of like tic-tac-toe, as we say. They're good at the tic and the tac, but the toe has been missing."

The power play has long been a useful tool for the offense to generate a quick score and change the momentum of a hockey game. The guys who are assigned to skate on the power play are expected to be the top offensive players, the most talented skill people, on the team. This is where those players want to be aggressive and put the puck in the net.

Mario Tremblay expressed his views on the importance of execution on the power play. "On the power play you don't need to have the giant shot, you just need to get the puck through and keep the forwards on the attack. The guys up front need to be looking for rebounds and you need to make sure everybody is working hard down low. A good power play team will try to keep one man in front of the goalie at all times. When the shot goes through, that player will act as a screen and try to shield the goalie from seeing the puck." He may also be looking for a deflection or tip-in, Tremblay said, as well as a rebound opportunity.

The Wild had the lowest power play conversion rate in the league, less than 10%, and that clearly has to improve. Jacques Lemaire knows that, and gives the impression that he relishes the challenge. "We need to convert on the power play with more frequency, that's for sure," he says. As he speaks he gets a look in his eye that makes one think that change may indeed come to the Wild power play units. "It's a priority for us."

It needs to be a priority, although scoring league-wide on the power play has dropped significantly from what it was in the early 1990's. One day up in the press box late in the season, a Detroit scout was talking about the Wild performance with the man advantage, and he laughed when he said; "They've got guys out there on the power play with seven goals, with 12 goals. And it's the 76th game of the year! We're awfully far into the season to have guys out there with those numbers."

Earlier in the year, Lemaire had spoken of how the power play would provide a special opportunity for the new guys. Players arriving to join the Minnesota Wild were told up front that there would be an opportunity to make an impact on special teams. When you build a new team, players who have never been on a power play with any regularity suddenly find themselves with the chance to step up. It is an opportunity to shine. The same goes for killing penalties, something the defense-oriented Wild has proven to be very good at. Lemaire still has some patience left for his offensive performers.

"You always feel that some of the guys will click and come up with the goal," says the man who scored 89 career power play goals during the regular season and an awesome 19 power play goals in the playoffs. "We didn't get that, we haven't gotten that on the power play. I know it's not just about one guy doing the job out there. You need more than that one guy. It's all about the teamwork, and sometimes it is a question of skill," Lemaire said.

He didn't sound disappointed when he spoke about the Wild's lack of scoring when they were a man up, but rather more resigned to the work that is sure to follow. The Wild have had a number of scoring opportunities that they just don't seem to finish. "I don't know," said Lemaire. "We've been practicing a lot, working on the power play in practice; we're trying to work on it all the time. You know, there are some things we do rather well, other things we don't do as well."

Lemaire pointed out that the Wild is not the only team struggling to score goals on the power play. The league is playing a lot of defense-oriented hockey, and it's probably not going to change in short order. "Defensemen are bigger and more mobile. You can't press them and force a lot of them to cough up the puck like the old days. Certainly, not as much. You know, I think they're much better, even from 20 years ago. With improved defense and better goalies, that's a big reason you are seeing less scoring around the league, especially on the power play."

"There are some teams who have superstars on the power play and they're just a few numbers ahead of us," added Lemaire. He laughed when informed of some dismal statistics, all of which place the Wild at the bottom of the league on the power play. "No, we're not satisfied. It takes a number of different things to go right to have a good power play, the right combination of people. You need to have the key man on the point, you need to have the playmaker, and the finisher. I've been really happy with the way we've been moving the puck, we've been getting chances. It's a matter of making the right play at the right time and getting the goal. The guys have been close."

Jacques Lemaire is a believer in his guys. He's not ready to quit on some of his young players who his instincts tell him are going to emerge as solid performers when the team has the man advantage. "Kuba's a good power play guy. Sekeras has been fine, and at the start of the year he scored a few goals. They will get better. We need to get more from the offense, we need to get more from the forwards. Some of the guys that have been there all year, Jimmy (Dowd) and Stacy (Roest) will have to step up. Gavey's been there too. But we need more from those guys. For a first year, I think Marian's been pretty good. Doug and I were talking about the power play this morning. This is exactly what we're trying to work on. We were talking about point men and about the type of guys we need up front. We'll be looking at some players."

TEN

THE BEST IN
THE GAME

The Pittsburgh Penguins came to town for a game on February 11, and the Minnesota Wild and their fans were ready for a battle. Mayor Norm Coleman gave the 'Let's Play Hockey' salute, and Minnesota Twins Hall of Famer Kirby Puckett had the honor of dropping the ceremonial puck. Mario Lemieux, the returned superstar, skated over to tap Kirby on the shoulder and have a warm exchange with the Hall of Fame outfielder. After a scoreless first period dominated by the Wild and highlighted by a scuffle between the elbow-throwing Darius Kasparaitis and Jim Dowd, it was Dowd who opened the scoring 3:30 into the second period by putting one in the net from the doorstep after a clean 2-on-1 break with Marian Gaborik. Pittsburgh answered with a breakaway goal from Robert Lang midway through the period, then Stacy Roest took a great feed from Roman Simicek, the former Pen, and rammed it home for a 2-1 Wild lead after two.

The Wild had succeeded in making the Penguins play their type of game through two periods, frustrating the potent Pittsburgh offense and outshooting the visitors 22-16 entering the final session. The Wild, who didn't take a penalty in the second period, took a 3-1 lead after Jaromir Jagr lost the puck and Curtis Leschyshyn potted one on the transition. But Pittsburgh was flying, and Jamie McLennan responded by playing one of his best third periods of the year. He stopped a big Martin Straka shot during a flurry and stayed resilient as the Pens picked up the attack after Lang scored his second of the game to make it 3-2 with just over four minutes left. Pittsburgh was coming after the Wild now, and Lemieux made a length-of-the-ice rush with 2:30 remaining that had the frantic crowd at the Xcel Energy Center saying their prayers. He was weaving through traffic and muscling past the Wild defenders, only to have his backhand come up empty.

Pittsburgh had outshot the Wild 12-3 in the third when, with a minute left, they mustered their final thrust and tested the Wild defense one last time. It provided one of the season's great defensive sequences. Alexei Kovalev and Darby Hendrickson were fighting for the puck at the blue line, with a score to tie the game the only thing on the Penguin forward's mind. Kovalev fired a shot that Hendrickson blocked. He wound up and fired again, but Hendrickson blocked that shot as well, somehow wresting the puck away from Kovalev while battling the Penguin from his knees, tipping it over to Walz, who scored an empty netter with 33 seconds left on the clock. The fans went berserk, and a few moments later many watched as big number 66, Mario Lemieux skated off the ice and walked, defeated, toward the visitors locker room. Final score: Minnesota Wild 4, Pittsburgh Penguins 2.

The Pittsburgh game highlighted the fact that the Minnesota Wild were not going along with traditional notions of playing "expansion" style hockey. They gave Pittsburgh only their second loss when meeting with an NHL expansion team since the league expanded in 1970 (their other loss was to the Edmonton Oilers in 1980). They held Lemieux scoreless for only the second time in 19 games, and ended his point-scoring streak at nine games. As a team, the Wild had put together a record of 20-17-5-3 since October 27th and were flat-out playing good, solid hockey. When they woke up the morning after the Pittsburgh game, they trailed Edmonton for the eighth and final western conference playoff spot by only six points.

Mario Lemieux came to meet the Minnesota press on a Sunday morning, entering through a side door that connected the visitors' locker room to the waiting media throng, which numbered about 35 by my count. I saw him coming from my perch near the rear of the room, and was impressed by his size and the athletic swagger he showed as he moved like a heavyweight title contender toward the assembled horde, finally gaining a position from which he could answer the usual questions about his return to hockey. "Superstar" is a term that is overused, but in this case the word is appropriate.

Dressed casually for this encounter with the press, wearing soft sandals and an easy smile, Mario had returned to the state of hockey that he once conquered before, in the 1991 Stanley Cup finals against the North Stars, won four games to two by Pittsburgh. Those games seemed like a long time ago, but Lemieux didn't look much different as he spoke, quietly yet firmly, on this Sunday morning. There was a trace of sweat gleaming on his forehead as the television lights bore down on him, though he looked at ease. He appeared big, of course, because he is; 6 feet 4 inches and 225 pounds of lithe muscularity that seems especially well proportioned. And he didn't look old, because he's not: 35 isn't terribly old for a highly talented professional hockey player. He looked to be in fighting trim and not a pound heavier than he needed to be.

His amazing start during the early days of his comeback was what intrigued me most. You would think that three years away from playing the game on the ice would necessitate a gradual return to form; perhaps not 100% of the old "Super Mario," but a steady, balanced growth into the superb level of play that he could reasonably be

Brad Bombardir, Kirby Puckett, and Jaromir Jagr.

expected to regain. That simply wasn't the case with this man. He had come back with fire and dominance, displaying sheer brilliance from the very start of the return on December 27. Coming into the Wild game at the Xcel Energy Center, Lemieux had garnered 17 goals and 18 assists in just 18 games. A fraction under two points a game was the best scoring average in the league during that time, and his 35 points would have tied him with Scott Pellerin for the Wild scoring lead.

The hockey world has been amazed by his performance, but this is a man who has come back from extraordinary challenges before. Minnesota fans remember the 1990-91 trip to the Stanley Cup finals, but do they remember that Mario Lemieux missed the first 50 games of that season because of complications following back surgery, returning to score 45 points in 26 regular-season games before stampeding through the playoffs? He scored 44 points in 23 playoff games, absolutely dominating his opponents as he ultimately led the Penguins past the North Stars 4-2 in that series.

Mario once suffered from Hodgkins disease and scored a goal on the very day he received his final radiation treatment, returning to win the NHL scoring title in 1993. He played just 22 games during the 1993-94 season, and sat out the 1994-95 season with a bad back, hoping to recuperate from his recent trials. He came back to win two more scoring titles, and the league MVP award, before announcing his retirement near the end of the 1996-97 season.

Lemieux had the privilege of being able to enjoy the company of some great offensive players when he returned to the Penguins in 2000-01, such powerful forwards as four-time Art Ross Trophy winner Jaromir Jagr, along with Robert Lang, Martin Straka and Alexei Kovalev. Those guys are some of the game's best, but Mario's presence only made them better and, most importantly, helped them to win more hockey games. Pittsburgh had been on a nice roll since Mario hit the ice, going 12-6 in the 18 games.

Additionally, all 18 games Lemieux had played in were sellouts, meaning he's the best box office draw in the game. Within 72 hours of the news of his return hitting the street, the Penguins sold 30,000 seats. Pittsburgh sold a single-day record 10,000 tickets the day before the official announcement of the comeback was made. With numbers like that, and the positive reception given to Mario's return around the NHL, the return of number 66 was nothing but great news artistically and financially for the league.

Lemieux is in most ways the opposite of the only other man who has so thoroughly dominated the game as he has: Wayne Gretzky. Take a look at the number that

Lemieux wears on his sweater—number 66, the reverse of The Great One's number 99. Lemieux came to the NHL after Gretzky had established himself as the grandest of players on one of the greatest hockey teams of all time, the Edmonton Oilers. When Lemieux revealed himself to be the offensive equal of Gretzky during the 1987 Canada Cup, people were reluctant to give Mario his due. Wayne came first and set the high standard, and even if Mario could challenge that level of excellence, there was also the matter of Mario's gaining acceptance from the English-speaking Canadians who revered the gift that was Gretzky. They are both icons of the highest order in Canada, and with Wayne retired, permanently, the spotlight shines alone on number 66.

Mario Lemieux was born in 1965 and grew up in a suburb of Montreal, not too far from Jacques Lemaire's childhood home. When Lemieux arrived in Pittsburgh in 1984, he could only answer questions in English with difficulty. There is a story that Mario honed his English speaking skills by watching soap operas on television. In whatever manner he learned, he is a fine speaker now, although the questions he is asked about his return are usually as repetitive as a Berlitz course. It's a wonder that he is able to endure the same questions that he must hear over and over when he hits a new town. There are a limited number of variations on the "what's it like to be back?" line of questioning. The people who are asking the questions are likely capable of better inquiries, but these are the same questions that always get asked in every city. Lemieux easily maintains a grace during the interview session that belies any distaste for the repetitive journalistic proceedings.

Moving down to the Zamboni area some time after the press conference, I watched Lemieux warm up with the rest of the Pittsburgh team. He's always easy to spot, standing something like 6' 7" on skates, with graceful moves as he swoops in on the net. Easy movements of his wrist result in bullet like shots on the goalkeeper in warm-ups, and the crowd watching the pre-game ritual was enthralled. I turned to a man who was in the first bank of seats along the glass, and asked him how he managed to snag the first seat next to the Zamboni, right there in the front row.

"I spent $150.00 on this seat, and I now owe my wife a big night out," said Dave Lendzyk of Winnipeg. He was watching Lemieux intently, his face right up to the glass with a grin that let me know he was in his element. He also had quickly fallen in love with the Xcel Energy Center. "I've been to Calgary and Carolina and a few others, but this is the best arena I've ever been in. I've been walking around the building, and the views from up top are great." So, why didn't you sit up there? "I'm a guy from Canada, who never thought he would get a chance to see Mario play again, so this is very special for me. Jaromir Jagr's out there too, so this is going to be fantastic!"

We talked for a few more minutes about the return of "Super Mario," and I got to wondering how much Mario Lemieux's return to hockey had influenced Michael Jordan's thoughts on returning to basketball. There are some differences, not the least of which is the fact that Jordan is three years older than Lemieux. The two sporting legends are golf buddies, with Mario holding the edge on the links. I believe that Michael watched the success that Mario was having after his extended layoff from hockey, and thought that he could do the same in basketball.

I watched as Lemieux did some stretching while on the ice, bending and trying to get his back to loosen up before the game. It's a concern again, his back. He wouldn't talk much about it before the contest with the Wild, but it's the number one reason he retired over three years ago. There was a story in the paper on Saturday before the Sunday game that his back was troubling him. What a shame that the nagging injury

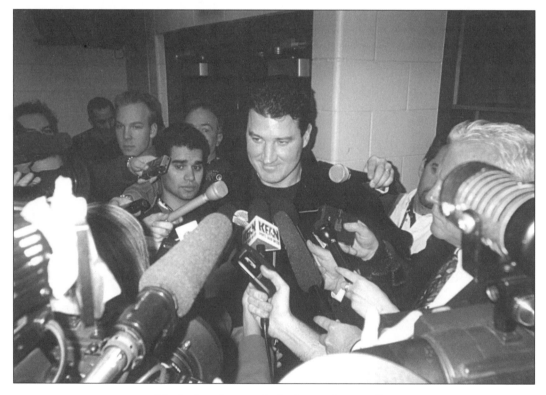

Mario Lemieux calmly faces the media.

was threatening to become an issue again. After the Wild game, Mario would say that his back was "…okay. I was not able to do some of the things I normally do, but I had to work with what I had."

Asked if he had felt better in the third period, when he was mixing it up pretty good, Lemieux said with a shrug, "I think starting in the second period I began to loosen up a little bit and feel a little better. A couple of Advil didn't hurt." I thought of my trips to the empty opponents' bench after games, and the litter of pain killers and paper cups scattered on the floor. They're just a band-aid to keep a player active, and not the cure so many wish Mario would find for his aching back.

In the first game between the two teams at the Xcel Energy Center, Lemieux had moments of control, but not the dominance that he had exhibited in some of the games since his return. He seemed to cover a little less ice than he used to, but he has always been a player who stays within himself and anticipates the puck. There's very little wasted movement by Mario Lemieux. He may be doing exactly as he wants, but with defenders dogging him when he even sniffs the puck, you can see what he is up against; when a man is such a giant on skates and cruises the front of the net like Jaws looking for a meal, he's always going to be a presence that demands constant hounding. The Wild held him to a handful of shots and only a couple of good scoring chances during the contest, including the impressive third period rush up the ice.

I caught Mario as he was moving through the corridor for the bus to the airport, and he seemed to recognize me from the earlier conference. He slowed, and allowed me to ask him a question that had nagged at me; how much of the comeback was truly inspired by the desire to have your son understand your role as a player in the game. He stopped momentarily and said, "It was a factor, there's no doubt about that. He didn't remember anything about my experience in the game, so it's nice to see him enjoying things as much as he has."

There was a lot more "trap" fallout than usual following the Pittsburgh game. The moaning coming from the Pittsburgh locker room after the 4-2 loss to the Wild was the most extreme of any team that came into the "X" all year. You had the equipment man telling a journalist that the game was a "farce," and the beat writer for the Pittsburgh Post Gazette calling the game "the most boring hockey game I've seen all year. It's not hockey the way it should be played at this level." It seemed like there were a lot of sour grapes coming out of the Pittsburgh locker room that night.

Mario tried to be diplomatic in his post-game comments, but he couldn't hide his frustration with the Minnesota style of defense. "Most of (Minnesota's) guys have been in the league for a while. Their team is very patient, and obviously they play the trap very well. They wait for their chance, they're well coached, and some of these guys have been around the game."

Then he uttered the comment that would mildly irritate Wild fans and players, as well as the hockey braintrust. When asked if there was too much clutching and grabbing going on, he responded: "Yes, especially tonight there were times I was very restricted, and that's not what we're trying to sell." Jacques Lemaire responded to that comment by saying, "I'd come out of retirement too, if no one was allowed to check me or play tough defense."

Perhaps the big offensive talents from around the league believe that the upstart Minnesota Wild should just stand around and watch while they put on a goal-scoring display for the fans in order to "sell the game."

Adding further fuel to the fire was a Kevin Stevens' remark: "If that's the way they have to play, it's too bad. It was nothing to write home about. It's no fun playing that way, but that's the way they do it. They won so they've got to be happy."

Lemaire's candid response was, "He should just shut up and be happy he's in the league and playing with someone like Lemieux."

Stevens, who scored 123 points with 54 goals for the Penguins during the 1991-92 season, and 111 points with 55 goals the following year, had seen his career hit a steep decline. Lemaire's comments were a veiled reference to Stevens' return to Pittsburgh after a journey around the league that ended with a suspension during the 1999-00 season.

With Mario, it's a little different. It hurts to hear one of the game's great leaders criticize the home team's style of play. But look at what he said, that he was restricted by the Wild defense. Well, that's exactly the Wild game plan. The goal of the defense has to be to restrict one of the greatest players in the game from doing his thing in the offensive end. And Lemieux himself noted after the game that "we do have to show a little bit more emotion out there."

That is what the Wild are doing; they are playing with intensity and emotion and making veteran teams, who aren't playing with fire, pay for that mistake. As far as what the league is "trying to sell," the NHL is not in the business of dictating how teams develop winning strategies. The Minnesota Wild did what they had to do to beat a fine Pittsburgh team that is much improved by the presence of Mario Lemieux.

Lemieux had some nice things to say about Minnesota hockey fans and the Xcel Energy Center as well. "They are great fans," Lemieux said. "They were great fans in the early '90's when we played them in the finals. They were the loudest in the league. It's nice to see they're selling out every game. Minnesota's a place that has deserved a hockey team for a long time, and I think they'll be here a long time."

The Minnesota Wild were beginning to experience some success, and it was in large part due to their strong defense. They were playing tough, tenacious "D" in most contests, and their success was drawing attention to their style of play. Some teams complained about the "neutral-zone trap" that was stifling their offense, especially after losses to a Wild team that hadn't existed a year before. The loudest complainers were the Pittsburgh Penguins after being stuffed by the Wild 4-2, but they were not alone.

The game against the Penguins drew a lot of attention to the fact that a few teams seemed to resent the Wild's brand of tenacious defense. The fact that the Wild were stifling the exciting comeback of Mario Lemieux was a big part of Pittsburgh's problem, and to the Wild, it sounded like so much whining. For the Wild organization, the shut-down of Super Mario was a telling tribute to their solid execution of the "1-2-2" defense.

Even Wild CEO Jac Sperling had something to say about the rampant belly-aching. "People seem to want to say that we are an expansion team playing this trap defense to stay in games. When Pittsburgh plays New Jersey, they don't say anything about facing a trap when they get beat. But when they come into our place and lose to the Wild, that seems to be unacceptable and there's a lot of complaining."

A trapping style of defense begins with the lead forechecker attacking the player who's bringing the puck up the ice and forcing him to one side or the other along the boards. Other players jam up the passing lanes, and a second forechecker keys the man awaiting the pass on that side of the half-board. Any kind of a cross-ice pass at this point is very dangerous, and the puck handler, finding no one to pass to, is effectively "trapped" in the neutral zone by the opposition. If a pass is errant or well defended, a turnover can occur, and that is when the Wild offense looks to break out and attack.

Los Angeles Kings coach Andy Murray, who used to coach at Shattuck St. Mary's in Faribault, was one of those quick to defend the Wild. "I like the way Jacques

Lemaire handles criticism of their style of play. He states that his team plays hockey as best they know how. They work so hard and have a very disciplined team on the ice. That's the key; they play hard and have gotten some excellent goaltending."

Lemaire probably takes too much heat for introducing the trap to the game of hockey. There have been defensive styles of play that involve the forechecker attacking the puck for many years, with the Montreal Canadiens foremost among them. But it was Jacques Lemaire who was able to hoist the Stanley Cup when he won the title with New Jersey in 1995, and that success seems to have come with the burden of being unfairly recognized around the league as the founder of the neutral-zone trap. Jacques simply teaches his players a more effective style of defense, the use of positioning to deny smooth offensive movement, and while he gets some credit for his efforts, he also takes a lot of flack. His players say that's not right.

"Jacques wants us to jump at the opportunities that are presented, and he gets upset if he thinks we're sagging back too much," said Darby Hendrickson. "The guys on other teams I've talked to, who have played against us, say that we play with a lot of discipline. They know that we capitalize on mistakes and are always looking to jump the other way.

"If we don't play aggressive hockey when we have opportunities on the offensive end, I guarantee you Jacques is not going to be happy, even if we keep the other team from scoring."

Jim Dowd feels that all the talk concerning the Wild's defensive approach is "…a joke. We have a great skating team and play solid hockey. We don't clutch and grab at all. All of a sudden we start winning some games and we're being judged by our style. It's just one of those things. I think we deserve credit for initiating plays and making things happen on the offensive end."

Early in the year, Jacques was quoted as saying that if a fan wanted to see lots of offense, "they should go see a basketball game." I think the occasional comment from Lemaire regarding his favored style of hockey comes from his frustration at having to constantly explain what to him is obvious: in this day and age of highly skilled players, top notch goaltending and consistently strong and increasingly technical coaching, it simply makes sense to keep things under control and capitalize on opportunities when they come. Thrust and parry.

Going up and down the ice like greyhounds may appeal to some hockey fans, but it's not the way the game is played by most teams in the league. And, more importantly, flying around the ice is not the best way to play winning hockey on a consistent basis. The bottom line is that teams who've lost to the Minnesota Wild, an expansion team, immediately search for an explanation for the defeat. The nearest straw to grab onto is the fact that Jacques Lemaire is coaching them and they must therefore be playing a sleepy, slowdown brand of hockey that no true NHL team would enjoy playing. That's just not the case.

Neal Broten, for one, thinks that the criticism of Lemaire and the style of play that he endorses, is misdirected. "I played in his system with New Jersey for a couple of years and I know that those who say that Jacques doesn't care about offense and goal scoring are wrong," said the former Stanley Cup champion. "There's room for offense and Jacques encourages it. He does believe that you can create offense with good, solid defense." Broten was proof of that in his time with the Devils during the Cup run of

Tough Defense or the "Trap?"

The Chicago Blackhawks were among the first to publicly attribute their lack of fire to the Wild's deployment of the dreaded trap. Now deposed coach Alpo Suhonen was barking his displeasure after a 5-2 beating laid on the Blackhawks by the Wild in Chicago on November 10th. The Minnesotans had goals from five different players during the contest, all at even strength, and simply outworked the Hawks in their own building. "Sometimes it seems like the best way to excuse your own team's performance is to blame the other guy's style of play," said Wild GM Doug Risebrough, referring to the Chicago game. "I find it laughable that, after they take a bad loss at home, our defense is supposed to be responsible for their lack of effort. That's not how it works in this game." Risebrough was having a hard time suppressing a smile, clearly enjoying Chicago's offensive discomfort. The Wild beat Chicago three of the four times they played.

The term "trap" has become a kind of nasty word around the NHL, used generically to explain the success the Wild was having against more established teams, who in most cases had been outworked and outhustled and didn't want to admit it. Jacques Lemaire believes in playing a "positionally smart" style of hockey that allows for offensive thrusts and counters. And, while a defensive focus can't be denied, Lemaire is not happy when the team is thinking only of defense.

1995. He had seven goals and twelve assists in 20 playoff games for Lemaire and New Jersey on the way to having his name engraved on Lord Stanley's Cup.

There are a number of teams around the NHL playing some version of the Wild's defensive style, including many of the best teams in the league. New Jersey plays it to near-perfection, but teams such as Dallas, St. Louis and Buffalo are also among the teams generally acknowleged to play defense in such a way that they reduce the ice avaliable for passing. They may not play that style with the same discipline that Jacques Lemaire demands of his players, but they do play it.

Even Colorado plays it tight. Watch the Avs in action and note the lead forechecker, frequently Chris Drury, Peter Forsberg or Sakic himself, attacking the man with the puck. There may be a difference in that the second forechecker doesn't seal the man off along the boards, making the Avalanche version more of a "one and a half," but it is still a defensive style designed to control the movement of the puck.

ELEVEN

THE NETMINDERS

It was three full months between victories for Jamie McLennan. He'd won the first game in franchise history when the Wild defeated Tampa Bay 6-5 at the Xcel Energy Center on the evening of October 18, a time when the leaves were changing on the trees and Americans were yet to head to the polls for a soon-to-be controversial Presidential election. Fifteen games in the net later, in the dead of a Minnesota winter, he successfully glided between the pipes again as the Wild defeated the New York Islanders 3-2 on January 19.

McLennan was in good humor after the game. "I'd told the guys I was going to go home and take a bath with the toaster," he said, regarding the long stretch that had yielded six ties to go with nine defeats. "This was a big personal win for me."

The Wild jumped out to a 3-0 lead, all three goals coming in the second period, from Darby Hendrickson, Antti Laaksonen and Wes Walz. After the Islanders scored two goals in the third period, they kept the pressure on to the finish, with Dave Scatchard hitting a pipe with 6:38 to play, as the New Yorkers outshot the Wild 11-5 in the final session. McLennan was up to the challenge on several other chances.

A telling statistic is this; through the Islander game, Minnesota had scored 61 goals in 28 games with Manny Fernandez in the lineup. With McLennan in the net, the team had scored just 27 goals in 21 games. It's a credit to Jamie that he has kept a positive attitude regarding the whole thing; he doesn't whine or gripe about his circumstances. "I knew something would break eventually," McLennan said after the win.

There was a pronounced feeling of relief among his teammates, who shared in the victory. Wes Walz, who played junior hockey for the Lethbridge Hurricanes of the WHL with McLennan, said, "The guys in the dressing room all love Jamie. He's a competitor, and if you don't know him well he may not come across as that kind of *guy, because he loves to joke around. I know him well and it was driving him crazy that he didn't have a win for all this time."*

A great goalie can make it happen, and there is a growing belief among some hockey people that the Wild's other goalie, Manny Fernandez, may someday be at the highest level. He has to prove it, of course, and therein lies the challenge: to establish himself as a player whose name will be remembered along with the names of the best netminders in the game.

The names of the great ones are as permanent as the ages, goalies like Terry Sawchuk, whose intense disposition made him vulnerable to the stresses of hockey's most difficult position, yet who still recorded more wins and posted more shut-outs than any other goalie in history. In the 1952 playoffs Sawchuk helped Detroit win the Stanley Cup with eight straight victories in two series while recording four shutouts and a 0.63 goals-against average, which is a modern record. And Ken Dryden, a brilliant man who led the Montreal Canadiens to six Stanley Cup championships in just eight seasons, leaving the game in his prime at age 31 to earn a law degree and write the award winning book, "The Game." He currently serves as president of the Toronto Maple Leafs.

Glenn Hall played 18 NHL seasons, becoming physically ill before almost every game that he played due to stress; he still holds the record of an incredible 502 consecutive games played. Johnny Bower was a journeyman professional, playing with the AHL's Cleveland Barons for eight years before becoming a champion with the Toronto Maple Leafs *15 years* into his career.

Tony Esposito, playing for the Chicago Blackhawks and often referred to as Phil Esposito's little brother, was the best goalie that I ever saw, though he never won the Cup. Something about a big goal by Jacques Lemaire in game seven of the 1971 finals that fired up the Canadiens and denied "Espo" a ring.

Goalies are guys who—voluntarily—go out night after night and act as targets for frozen, hard-rubber missiles that are sent their way at speeds often exceeding 100 mph. Yeah, they're well-padded, but it's still a dangerous and, to most folks, very scary way to earn a living. And it was even tougher before the invention of facemasks and high-tech protective materials. Yet these guys not only do it, they absolutely love it! And how about the hundreds of guys who played goalie before facemasks were invented? Hall, Bower and Sawchuk were fearless without the facemask, and Gump Worsley, who finished his quarter-century professional career with the North Stars, played all but his last year (1973-74) without one.

So, goalies ain't normal. A lot of us already know that. How can we say it politely? "Netminders have nuances?" That sounds better, doesn't it? Goalies have got some ways about them that are, well, unique. Having said that, we need to face the truth about NHL hockey today. It all begins with the guy between the pipes. No team in the National Hockey League is able to make it far these days without a superior goalie. Even the Colorado Avalanche, which has an outstanding offensive team, depended on a great backstop to complement its scoring punch. Patrick Roy just won an unprecedented third Stanley Cup MVP award and showed himself, once again, to be the best of the best in the net.

Martin Brodeur, the goalie for the New Jersey Devils, defeated the Wild twice during the inaugural season, giving up two goals in each game and stopping 46 of 50 shots in the pair of matchups. The Wild put some pressure on Brodeur during their first meeting in St. Paul, outshooting New Jersey 22-21 for the night. Brodeur thought the Wild played with a lot of confidence for a young team, saying after the game that "it looks like they have Jacques' system down pretty good. It will be a matter of time for them to mature and keep getting better."

Brodeur plays solid goal for the Devils, and grew up the son of a Canadian Olympian (father Denis, 1956) who played minor league baseball in North Dakota. As Martin advanced as a goalie he admired and emulated Colorado's Patrick Roy. What is interesting is that Brodeur seems to play in the shadow of Roy, never commanding the respect of the Avalanche star, despite having won two Stanley Cups. The 2001 Cup final was a showdown between Brodeur and Roy, a battle won by Roy as the Avalanche won the Cup in seven games. While Brodeur gave up a stingy 2.07 goals per game during 25 playoff games, he was bested by Roy's 1.70 GAA during the run for the Cup.

Emmanuel "Manny" Fernandez has the potential to be a great goaltender, and some would say he showed exceptional skills in the net during the inaugural season. He's been a winner for all of his hockey life, picking up a gold medal with the 1994 Canadian National Junior team and making the playoffs in each of his five seasons in the International Hockey League. He played with the Houston Aeros of the IHL in 1998-99, where he posted an impressive 36-6-9 record and won the Turner Cup.

Manny looked at his trade from Dallas to the Wild as a demotion when Doug

Risebrough acquired him in the deal with the Stars' GM Bob Gainey. "How else could I look at it at the time?" recalled Fernandez. "The Stars were winners and I had friends there; I wasn't sure what the situation would be in Minnesota."

That is understandable. The young goalie had tasted the big time while with the Stars, playing in the Stanley Cup finals and gaining a friend and mentor in the great (but not altogether normal) Eddie Belfour, who was suspended in January of 2001 for temporarily walking out on his team because he was unhappy. Fernandez is quick to credit Belfour with helping to develop the technical aspects of his game. Backing up Eddie the Eagle was a learning experience for Fernandez, a time for study and growth. He tasted victory and had the experience of playing for a great hockey team.

Doug Risebrough is a big fan of strong netminders, and he shared the story of the Wild's procurement of goalie Manny Fernandez. "Acquiring Manny was a relationship thing that worked out well for us," said Risebrough. "We had all of our people going to look at him when Eddie Belfour was hurt (during the 1999-2000 season).

"One of my friends in the business is Bob Gainey, and I asked him to let me know when we could talk about Manny, because he was busy getting ready to go to the Cup. Bob was very positive about Manny, about the person who is Manny Fernandez. Some guys, you really worry about their positive comments. It's kind of like a used car salesman telling you not to worry about a little dent in the car when actually the whole frame is bent," Risebrough said with a grin.

While Doug was enjoying his comparison to the used car salesman, he quickly wanted to make it clear he wasn't referring to his friends in the business.

"I went to see game five of the Dallas Stars-Colorado Avalanche series and, though Manny wasn't playing, I was able to tell Bob (Gainey is a friend of Risebrough's from his Montreal days, as well as a former North Star and Hall of Famer) that he should tell me when we could talk trade. We wanted Manny, but were trying to be low key.

"The timing was important, because a year earlier Bob had a difficult time with back-up goalie Roman Turek, when just days after the playoffs ended he had to either trade the player or lose him to expansion. So I just said to him 'You tell me when you want to talk about this,' because I didn't want it to be confusing. News like that, if it ever leaked out, could cause trouble. Here you are going to the Stanley Cup Finals and word gets out about a trade: that could be disastrous. When the season was over he would have a little more time to play with."

Ultimately, it was a relatively straightforward two-component deal that ended up with Manny Fernandez, Pavel Patera and Aaron Gavey wearing Minnesota Wild uniforms in exchange for two 3rd-round draft picks! Doug Risebrough would be formidable himself out on the used-car lot!

The Wild netminder was owned by Dallas for six seasons and played in 33 NHL games for the Stars, 24 during the 1999-2000 season. Belfour taught him professionalism and showmanship, as well as the intensity and fearlessness that helped Manny to win 19 games with the Wild in 2000-01. Fernandez has put his education with Eddie and the Stars to good use with his new team, not least in his exceptional performance against his old squad in the 6-0 Minnesota victory over Dallas on December 17 at the Xcel Energy Center. He closed the season with an outstanding 2.24 goals-against average and a .920 save percentage, placing him in the top ten in the league in both statistical categories.

Fernandez is gaining consistency as he matures in the game that he has loved since he was a very young goalie growing up in Ontario, fielding shots from his mom, Muguette Fernandez—Manny says he's been playing hockey since he was two years old. He has exhibited the athletic grace of his butterfly style on numerous occasions, a goaltending technique he shares with many French-Canadian netminders. It's a manner of stopping the puck with flourish, getting down low to make saves that more vertical goalies often miss, especially with traffic in front of the net.

It's a style that has made him the Wild's most effective goalie and that helped him to notch four shutouts while putting together an extraordinary eight-game unbeaten streak that lasted from December 7, 2000 to January 10, 2001. Manny played in 42 games for a total of 2,461 minutes with the Wild during the team's inaugural season, and he would have played more if not for a bum ankle that cost him time in October and at the end of the year.

There's no question that Jamie McLennan comes to play hard every single night he steps out on the ice. But is there anything to the lack of offensive support that he seemed to fall victim to time and again during the Wild's first season? There is thinking in some quarters that McLennan is the type of "solid citizen" the Wild want to have to back up Manny Fernandez. "Noodles," as McLennan is affectionately known, was a very positive presence in the locker room and a solid goalie, but at some point you are forced to look at the raw numbers. Jamie went 5-23-9 on the year, though performing much better than his record indicated. Still, the win-loss ratio was not good.

A west-coast scout who saw a number of Minnesota's games felt that Fernandez

Jim Mattson: A Goalie Forever

Jim Mattson played goalie for the Minnesota Golden Gophers back in the 1950's, and was recently named as one of the 50 greatest players of all time at the University. He still carries the record for lowest goals against average at the school (2.37 over his career) and is tied for the most shutouts ever. "He was a whale of a goalie," recalled former North Star coach Glen Sonmor. "He's from the old school of guys who grew up playing without the great equipment, but played for love of the game."

In fact, he grew up playing with flight boots protecting his feet on the ice, and a piece of lath as his stick. That's how you did it when you were growing up in St. Louis Park, Minnesota without a lot of money. Jimmy is still supremely confident in the skills that took him to a pair of WCHA titles and to the national championship game on two occasions. He still plays four nights a week while living in Indiana, and he thinks he could help the right professional team. "I would like to try out and see where I stand. I'm pretty sure I could get the job done or I wouldn't be out there asking for a look." Yes, Jimmy's gotta be in his 60's, but he's earnest in his belief that he could still play at a high level!

Jimmy was a teammate of the great John Mayasich, a Minnesotan whom he described as "one of the true greats. John played with control and finesse that was ahead of his time, plus he was a great athlete. He had a little move where he would flip the puck over an opponents stick and come flying out of there on the break. He was good, we were good, and we should have won the nation."

Mattson also remembers watching Glen Sonmor play on a line with Frank King and Wally Hargesheimer with the Minneapolis Millers of the old USHL in the late 40's. "That was a pretty darned good line they had there. All those guys spent some time in the NHL." While in high school he would "just show up" and practice with those players, recalls Sonmor, taking shots from the pros and "always working on his game."

"I've always loved hockey," says Mattson. "As long as I can remember, I've been a goalie."

was the goalie the Wild could count on the most to make the essential saves that keep teams in hockey games. "I didn't think that Manny Fernandez made all that many 'highlight reel' saves," the scout said, "at least during the games that I saw. What he did, though, was make the saves that you need to make with great consistency. You need your guy to make the saves that keep you in it.

"I think Manny did that a little better than Jamie," continued the scout. "It seemed like there were a few occasions where McLennan didn't make the big save. For some guys it's easier to play in goal when their team is behind. I personally thought Jamie played better when the Wild were trailing."

His thinking is that Manny played more consistently in the net, regardless of whether the Wild were up or down on the scoreboard. And Fernandez did give a very consistent performance in the games that he was in, although he missed a number of games with injuries. McLennan stepped in and fought the battle when he was asked to and displayed class despite the adversity that came with a frequent lack of offensive support.

Jacques Lemaire liked the job that both of his goalies did for the team over the course of the year. "I would say that they both played very well. They each played about the same number of games (McLennan 38 and Fernandez 42 games played). We didn't support Jamie as well with goals, but I don't know why that is."

Lemaire credits the improvement in the play of the netminders with the most fundamental changes in the game today. "The guys who were the scorers in my day would still get their goals, players like Steve Shutt and Guy Lafleur. But the goalies are improved from our time, no doubt about that.

"Goalies today study every angle, every move on the ice," continued Lemaire. "They look for any play that could be made by the offensive man, and they work on stopping it. They practice to take away any offensive advantage. There's a lot of teaching. In the past it was more 'If you don't stop the puck, you don't play.' Now there's more to it."

Some guys who play the position are battlers, and that's how Doug Risebrough views McLennan, a six-footer from Edmonton, Alberta. "Jamie wants to be in there all the time. He's at his best when he goes after it and plays aggressively," said Risebrough. "I feel the competition has benefitted our goalies.

"This was not a bad team to play in front of; they check so well in their own zone and position themselves so well that they didn't get barraged for long periods of time.

But clearly there were games where they were under siege for a given time and that's when you really need a strong goalie. Manny came through big in a lot of games for us and so did Jamie."

Risebrough has some ideas about the challenge that is inherent to playing goalie in the NHL. He knows that the job is not easy, and that only a certain kind of individual will thrive under the pressure. "Goalies are generally really intense people who need to build in their own mechanisms for evaluating themselves, because not a lot of people can legitimately judge their game," said Risebrough. "I have to admit myself that, after watching a goalie play a tough shot and give up a score, I'm not often sure if it was a 'bad' or 'good' goal based on all the circumstances."

Goalies have to become good self-critics and monitor themselves; only the goalie truly knows just where he is mentally. The net can be a very lonely place on the ice when things are tough. "Quite often the only support a goalie has is himself, or the back-up goalie who taps him on the pads once in a while for encouragement," says Risebrough. "But I think goalies are generally bright, intuitively smart people. It's a tough position to play in the NHL. If confidence is what takes a goalie to another level, that confidence can also be taken away very quickly by other people's mistakes. And if they're out of sync, they know it before anybody else knows it."

So there is that balancing that goes on, that fine line that goalies walk; confidence, a certain cockiness, on the one hand, and yet on the other, the realization of how quickly that can be taken away. When a few things go wrong, even when it's not necessarily the goalie's fault, it can all disappear. The psychological battle is a full-time job that can't be overworked, it has to be waged subtly on many fronts.

Manny, who is the nephew of coach Jacques Lemaire, doesn't mirror his uncle's more reserved style, but he seems to have the same ability to see through the tough times, the occasional bad game, and not let it affect the game ahead. He's one of the more articulate of the Wild players around the locker room, usually available to answer questions from the media with a generally patient disposition, though he has a nature that could be construed as confidence bordering on cockiness. That's part of the deal with Manny Fernandez, and with goaltenders in general. Maintaining confidence is an indispensable part of their game.

When I spoke to Manny just after the All-Star game, I noted that the goalies in the contest had been roughed up a bit. Martin Brodeur, for one, had given up several goals in just a few minutes of play. I asked Fernandez, "Would it be worth it to you to sacrifice your days off during the break and take that kind of punishment just to be an All–Star?"

Manny didn't hesitate. "Absolutely," he answered. "Any time you have a chance to be an All–Star, you want to be there. No question about it." Then he gave a writer a look that would have melted ice for asking such a dumb question.

Although he had stated in the media that he didn't care about All–Star consideration, and noted that he was sharing the Wild goaltender's job with McLennan, some journalists felt Fernandez could have been in the big game, and there was talk right to the end that he would be added to the team. Tradition has dictated that each team send a representative to the game, although there is no official league rule. Ultimately, there was no Minnesota representative. When he didn't make the squad, he would not admit that he was disappointed. But why shouldn't he be?

He had led the fledgling franchise to some tremendous victories and a certain respectability around the league, and there had traditionally been a player taken from each team to be a representative at the game. For many fans, media types and members of the Wild organization, Fernandez was the choice to head to Denver and symbolize the Minnesota Wild at the festivities.

McLennan missed one game in November and was out four games in early March. Fernandez's leg injuries kept him out of 18 games for the year. On a couple of occasions McLennan was called into action without a lot of warning, a challenge for any goalie who values his preparation time. Early in the season he was pressed into action for a Sunday matinee game against the Edmonton Oilers after Manny went down with an ankle injury, and he didn't have a good game as the Wild lost 5-3. It was McLennan's first loss of the season, and he would make no attempt to shirk the blame.

"Any time you're not scheduled to start, it's a little surprise," McLennan said after the game. "There are no excuses. It's a situation where you have to respond and give the team a chance to win. There were some untimely goals and mental errors on my part (including a first period McLennan turnover, which led to the Oilers' first score). That was the difference in the hockey game."

You have to respect a guy whose nature is to stand up and take responsibility for a team loss. Three days later McLennan would play solidly and notch the first-ever Wild victory, a 6-5 win over Tampa Bay in the sixth game of the season at the Xcel Energy Center. Although he gave up three goals late in the game, the Wild held on for a thrilling victory behind Marian Gaborik's late goals at 17:32 and 19:02 of the third.

In McLennan's favor is the fact that he usually played strong in the net despite the team's lack of offensive punch when he played. After stopping 30 of 33 shots in a 3-1 loss to the San Jose Sharks, he was unbeaten in the next two games, stopping 57 of 59 shots in a pair of ties.

The first tie came in a game with Florida, a scoreless duel against a potent offense, including a great stop of a Pavel Bure breakaway. Bure made a one-on-one move about five minutes into the game, which was neatly poked away by McLennan, a critical play early in the contest. He made 20 saves, a number of them tough, and the Wild owned the overtime, taking five shots to the Panthers' zero, but the home team couldn't score the winner. Of the Bure save, Jamie said "He's such a great scorer you do what you can; sometimes a little luck comes into play." It didn't seem to be luck on the Bure save, however, just a great play early in what would be a tight game.

Then the Wild tied Montreal 2-2 at "Le Centre Molson" (The Molson Center—not quite the same ring to it as "The Montreal Forum") to gain their first-ever point on the road. Jamie made 33 saves, and was close to a win before Eric Weinrich tied it up late. Those two gems were followed by a lousy outing against Toronto.

After the drought-ending victory in January over the Islanders, Wild captain

Jamie McLennan: a shutout.

Behind the Mask

Manny Fernandez parallels Eddie Belfour in more ways than just style of play. Both players use masks painted by a master of the art, Todd Miska, a native Minnesotan who, although he never played hockey as a youth, now creates 150 masks a year for goaltenders at all levels. Miska and Fernandez hooked up for a total of six hours before the season started to get it just right. Manny's mask is a ferocious animal face in a collage of colors with emphasis on reds, greens and golds.

The goaltender's mask today is as comprehensive and protective as a motorcycle helmet, only more custom-fitted. Moldmaker Dom Malerba uses a process that involves covering the face of the person being fitted with Saran Wrap and coating it with plaster of paris; the goalie can't move for the 20 minutes it takes to harden.

To say the mask reflects a goaltender's personality is an understatement; the mask is a reflection and an expression of what thoughts are going on behind the face-protector. Belfour has the logo of his favorite charity, the Make-A Wish Foundation, on the chin of his mask, which has a finely detailed eagle as its main frontal feature and race cars on the backplate. Fernandez has the number 31 on his backplate as a tribute to the late, great Philadelphia Flyer goalie Pelle Lindbergh, who was killed tragically in a car crash. "I thought he was a great goalie," said Fernandez. "I watched him a lot when I was young and learned things from him." His mask also features blue colored eyes on the face of the animal portrayed on the front, a nod to another mentor, "Eddie the Eagle" Belfour.

Brad Bombardir said, "We really wanted to go out and get a win for Jamie. He's played really well and we (the offense) haven't given him any breaks. I give him a lot of credit for hanging in there when things have been tough."

McLennan never complained about anything, except perhaps the officiating of one of Jacques' and Jamie's favorite referees (who may have cost him a game or two), and simply went right on battling to the end of the season. He earned the respect and admiration of his teammates and is regarded as a stand-up hockey player by everyone in the Wild locker room.

"It's not easy going out there and hoping that your team will score some goals for you," said Scott Pellerin in January. "We need to bust out for the guy and get some numbers on the board. I don't know what it is, but it's not lack of effort."

McLennan was not protected by St. Louis in the 2000 expansion draft despite a miniscule 1.96 goals against average and 9-5-2 record during the 1999-00 season with the President's Cup-winning Blues. The year before, he went 13-14-4 with a 2.38 GAA in 33 games, and during the 1997-98 campaign he was a very strong 16-8-2 with a 2.17 GAA while appearing in 30 contests. McLennan, who also played for the New York Islanders early in his NHL career, garnered some playoff experience during his years with St. Louis and showed himself to be a reliable force between the pipes, something the Minnesota Wild believed him to be.

Jamie McLennan proved himself to be a leader and a tough-minded team player for the Wild during the inaugural season. The hope here is that he gets another opportunity to put up some won-loss statistics that will bear out the type of winning netminder he can be.

TWELVE

WILD FIGHTERS

The Minnesota Wild's contest with the St. Louis Blues on March 14 was the first game they had played without the services of Curtis Leschyshyn, the defenseman who was traded to Ottawa for draft picks the previous day. He was moved just hours before the trading deadline was reached, the casualty of a situation in which Doug Risebrough felt he had to get something for a quality player who would become an unrestricted free agent at the end of the season. The move followed the trades of Scott Pellerin and Sean O'Donnell. Risebrough stayed with his strong belief that you build the core of a franchise through the entry draft, and he garnered a third-round pick for the solid Leschyshyn.

The hard-hitting defenseman made almost two million dollars playing for the Wild during the inaugural season, and had done a fine job of being a leader. He was tough on Mario Lemieux when the Penguins came to town on a roll and left with a 4-2 loss. He even scored a key goal in the game, one of his two on the season. By going to Ottawa, he would rejoin Senators coach Jacques Martin, with whom he'd won a Stanley Cup when they both were with Colorado in 1996. (Martin had been an assistant coach with the Avalanche. It should be noted that Ottawa would stumble badly, losing four straight to Toronto in the 2001 Cup quarterfinals.)

Leschyshyn ultimately enjoyed his time with the Wild, although he joined the team with some trepidation. "You hear expansion horror stories," Leschyshyn said after the trade. "I've had friends in this league who have played for expansion teams, and I can guarantee their experiences weren't as fulfilling as mine have been.

"I think the way the Minnesota Wild approached this season—the players they selected in the expansion draft, the trades they made early—shows that they want to be competitive and they really want to win. They don't want to sit around and be mediocre for any length of time."

Keeping Curtis Leschyshyn was cost prohibitive for a team that is trying to build with youth and to spend wisely. Defense is an area where the Wild feel pretty good about how the young guys are shaping up, and spending big money to keep an older veteran is not the way they're doing things at the club's St. Paul offices. Curtis was a solid player and a good fit, but not worth the dough that might be spent more wisely toward developing the hockey team.

After the exciting win over Pittsburgh at home on February 11, things started to get tougher for the Minnesota Wild. A visit to the Penguins three days later found a determined Mario Lemieux up to the challenge of evening things in the rematch, scoring both goals in a 2-1 Penguins victory at Mellon Arena. Wes Walz got things going for the Wild with one of his trademark shorthanded goals to open the scoring in the second period, but it was all Mario in the third as the Pens rolled to the win.

The Penguins outshot the Wild in the contest 35-14, and after having defeated Dallas and Pittsburgh back-to-back only days before, perhaps a letdown was to be expected. The Wild had finished a six-game stretch on the road with the 2-1 defeat of Dallas, netting nine of a possible twelve points during a stretch that wrapped around the All-Star break. Scott Pellerin thought that the Wild's success during the previous trip had been a highlight of their season. "We did what needed to be done, and we played through the challenges of the road. I think I went a few weeks without sleeping in my own bed, and it was good to be back home."

The Pittsburgh game cost the Wild more than just a loss, however. Darius Kasparaitis gave Darby Hendrickson a concussion with a suspect blind-side shot in the second period. The blow would take Hendrickson out of the Wild's next three games.

The loss to the Penguins wasn't a good performance by the team, and it was followed by a 4-0 shutout at the hands of goalie Jamie Storr and the Los Angeles Kings at home. After a 3-1 victory over the San Jose Sharks at the "X," the Wild went back on the road, dropping three straight—to Dallas (6-2), Colorado (4-1) and Nashville (2-1). The questions were beginning to mount regarding the future of some of the Wild's top performers who were due to become free agents at season's end. Scott Pellerin, Sean O'Donnell and Curtis Leschyshyn were all subject to trade talk that couldn't help but be a distraction to the focus of the team.

The Wild needed to try to play through what appeared to be the imminent loss of three of their best guys, and they did their best to 'talk the talk' while the rumor mills churned. "It's important that we keep our focus on the ice and keep playing hard, like we have all year," emphasized Hendrickson. "Things that are out of our control, well, there's not much we're going to be able to do about that stuff. We've got to keep playing the way we know how."

Hendrickson was right, of course, but the guys who were on the block were leaders on the young squad, veterans all, who had contributed mightily to the success of the first-year franchise. Pellerin was the leading scorer, and both Leschyshyn and O'Donnell were backbone-type defensive players who knew how to step up and play tough down the stretch in close games. The idea of losing hard-checking tough guys had to hurt, but no one on the Wild wanted to admit that fact. The attitude among the team was to muscle-up and battle.

After all, that was what they had done all year. With Vancouver in town on February 26, Minnesota sought to stop the three-game losing streak. The three losses in a row matched the team's longest losing streak of the year, but it was a rowdy crowd at the Xcel Energy Center on a frigid Monday night. "Sometimes the fans have created the atmosphere when we haven't," said Scott Pellerin. "I thought tonight might be one of those nights." The Wild threatened early when Wes Walz grabbed the puck in a shorthanded situation and skated in alone on Bob Essensa, but when the Canuck netminder made the save, Vancouver headed the other way in a hurry, with Scott Lachance notching a score at 3:45 of the first period.

Daniel Sedin added another goal for the Canucks a mere half-minute later, and then Pellerin came through with a power play goal on a top-shelf wrist shot off a feed from Marian Gaborik. Minnesota managed to tie the game early in the second period with another power play goal from Pellerin, but Todd Bertuzzi scored the eventual game winner three minutes later. The Wild never seriously threatened after that.

"It was one of those nights where nothing seemed to work out as well as it could have," said Walz later. "We were working hard, but it seemed like they were a step ahead of us all night." Vancouver was indeed a step ahead, as well as scoring chances ahead. The Wild were outshot by the visitors 12-6 in the first period, and finished the game trailing 32-17 in pucks on net. Final score: Vancouver 5, Minnesota 2.

Vancouver had come in hungry after losses to Toronto and Ottawa, determined to play better and elevate their game. "We needed a good win to get ourselves going. They play tough all the time, so it feels real good to get this one in our favor," said former Gopher and Wild nemesis Trent Klatt after the win. In late January, Klatt had complimented the Wild defense after a 3-2 overtime Canuck victory in Vancouver. "They get that first goal and, with the system they play, it allows them to almost suffocate you," said Klatt. "They make you beat all five guys and it's hard to penetrate. You're not going to beat them with odd-man rushes or fluke plays."

But beat them they did on this night, and the Wild had lost four in a row for the first time all year. A disallowed Wild goal in the third period brought out the season's first bad behavior by the fans—a flurry of plastic bottles hit the ice after Stacy Roest's apparent score was negated. Nobody on the Wild side was very pleased with this game, either. GM Doug Risebrough was seen leaning against the wall of his suite above the press box, hand up to his chin in a thoughtful pose at game's end. And the uncharacteristically irritated former Canuck Hendrickson commented, "We came out on our heels, and they've got some guys who can jump. That's not how we would like it to happen, but sometimes it goes that way."

Jacques Lemaire was a little edgy himself at the post-game press conference. "We've got some guys who come to play every night. Every night," Lemaire repeated. "Walz, Kuba, Hendrickson, and Laaksonen, those guys might have a shift here and there where they're off their game, but other than that..." his voice trailed off. "We have some guys who seem to play better when they have a little success early, but they have to come to play the whole game."

Jacques would come the closest he'd ever been to pointing the finger at a couple of his leaders. "I can accept when players have a bad game, and some of our better players have been off a little bit," said Lemaire. "Maybe some of the guys know that they're out of the playoffs and let up out on the ice." He didn't say it, but there was a sense that he felt a little frustration with players who knew that their remaining time with the Wild was limited.

"I'm disappointed," he said.

On a lighter note, Lemaire was somewhat baffled by "the birds and the bees." Aaron Gavey's wife, Jennifer, was due to give birth at any time, and Gavey had informed the coaching staff that he might need to leave for the hospital that evening. Before the game, Jacques was made aware of that fact by Mike Ramsey, who told him that Gavey could disappear during the contest. "You mean he might leave right in the middle of the game?" Lemaire asked incredulously. Yes, Ramsey had responded, he's going to leave as soon as he gets word that the delivery is under way. Jacques sent someone to check on the accuracy of this report and, once it was confirmed, he scratched Aaron and substituted another player. "I can't have a guy leaving right in the middle; I need a guy who can play the whole game," remarked Lemaire after the contest. Reminded that Darby Hendrickson's wife was due as well, Jacques sighed and said, "That's right. We might lose two guys. Hopefully we'll have enough left to play hockey."

After a tie at Calgary and a loss at Edmonton, the Wild extracted a measure of revenge on the Canucks on March 4 by defeating them 4-3 in overtime at General Motors Place. Aaron Gavey, back in the line-up after the late scratch in the previous meeting, scored the winning goal, unassisted, at 2:24 of overtime, ending the club's six-game winless streak. Minnesota managed to get things flowing right out of the gate for a change, scoring on three of their first 10 shots en route to a 3-0 lead just 12:24 into the game. Gavey also managed to score the first goal of the contest at the four-minute mark, his first score since potting one on January 30. The Wild followed with power play goals from Sergei Krivokrasov and Marian Gaborik before the Canucks made a game of it. It was the Wild's fourth overtime victory. Risebrough later described Gavey as "a gamer. He has a knack for turning up in the right place at the right time."

The victory had come without the services of either Scott Pellerin or Sean O'Donnell, who had been dealt to Carolina and New Jersey, respectively. The Wild were forced to make a move, as both players, along with Curtis Leschyshyn, were due to become unrestricted free agents after the season. The Wild tried to make a deal to keep Pellerin with the team, but negotiations reached a point of no return. O'Donnell told the Wild that he planned to test the free-agent market after the season, and thus also had to be moved so the Wild could secure something in return for him.

Scott Pellerin had been a key offensive force for the Wild and was widely considered the team's best player. He was always available to the media and took time to answer any question, usually providing a good quote. Hunched at his locker, he looked small in size, but he sure played big for the Wild. Scott had the splendid knack of being in the right place on the ice at the right time, a certain hockey savvy that not every player has, but most good players possess.

While at the University of Maine, Pellerin won the Hobey Baker Memorial Award as the top U.S collegiate player in 1992, and I know he liked the idea of the Minnesota

Wild housing the award. Pellerin used to say that he wanted a part of the Wild's future, but Scott seemed to want a better contract more than he wanted to stay with the Wild. That is certainly his right, but the fit with the Wild seemed so good. While making $935,000 with the inaugural Minnesota Wild squad, Pellerin had scored 11 goals and had 28 assists in 58 games. With the Carolina Hurricanes, he tallied no goals and five assists in 19 games, quite a drop-off. On a Minnesota team where a lot of pucks seemed to bounce off sticks, he held on to some rubber when it was needed and had a lot of big goals before he left. In the end, a nice contract and the proximity to his New Hampshire home landed him in Boston for 2001.

Sean O'Donnell scored 16 points in 63 games for the Wild, and just one point (an assist) in 17 games for the Devils. He endured his time in the Midwest with dignity and played with fire on a number of occasions. O'Donnell never thought he was going to end up in Minnesota to begin with; he had played 80 games in each of the previous three seasons for the Los Angeles Kings, and Kings general manager Dave Taylor had told him they would be able to make a deal to keep him in L.A., although he was eventually left unprotected in the expansion draft. Risebrough and the Wild foiled the King's plans by making Sean the first pick among defensemen. "I loved the building, the people of Minnesota and the whole experience here," said O'Donnell, on his way out the door. He was an asset to the team while he was here, the first player to wear the "C" on a Wild sweater, but he really did want to be in California or New York with actress-wife Allison Dunbar.

New team captain Darby Hendrickson downplayed the changes to the roster before the Wild's game against the St Louis Blues, saying, "We've just got to play hockey and not worry about who's here and who's not. That's an easy excuse for us to make, but it's not what we're about and I'll be very surprised if we come out with any less jump."

When the Wild took the ice against the Blues at the "X" on March 6, they had a different look and a fighting attitude. The Blues opened the scoring, with Ladislav Nagy netting a goal just two minutes into the contest. The Minnesotans responded with Wes Walz's shorthander four minutes later, and took a 2-1 lead on Marian Gaborik's 17th goal of the season late in the first period.

After a scoreless second the Blues, who were missing a few of their top players, including super defensemen Chris Pronger and Al MacInnis, and who had been injury-prone for most of the year, scored a couple of goals in the third to take a 3-2 lead. The Blues' second goal came after Andy Sutton of the Wild tossed a Blues player to the ice for no obvious good reason, leading to a Scott Young power play goal to tie the game. Dallas Drake then scored the leader on a nice assist from Pierre Turgeon. With the Blues' top defensemen off the ice, the Wild were better able to prowl around the St. Louis net, which eventually paid off on their 28th shot of the game, Cam Stewart scoring to tie the game with two minutes left.

The 3-3 final was more satisfying than most ties, in that the Wild had been forced to muscle-up and claw for the equalizer against a strong club. The 'Wildmation' scoreboard had shown the famous scene of John Belushi's Bluto from *Animal House* asking "Who's with me?" and it was Stewy who responded by grabbing a slip pass from Antti Laaksonen and slamming home the game-tying score past flailing Blues goalkeeper Brent Johnson. "My job's to go out and work hard and maybe cash in once in a while, so this was nice," said Stewart after the game.

St. Louis managed seven shots in the overtime to the Wild's two, but Manny Fernandez was up to the challenge and preserved the knotted score by making a couple of exceptional saves among his 32 for the night. The whole team had worked hard and managed a significant tie with playoff-bound St. Louis, the first home battle without Pellerin and O'Donnell, so this result was a heck of a lot better than a loss.

After the game, Blues coach Joel Quenneville showed the strain of his team's eight consecutive non-winning performances on the road. He was out in the hallway of the locker-room area doing an interview, trying to keep a positive attitude despite what must have been a rough tie for his club, when he finally came a bit undone. After finishing the on-air session, he turned to a fellow in the hallway and lit out—primarily at himself.

"I'm just freaking livid with myself for who I had out there on the ice," roared Quenneville. "I had the wrong bleeping guys out on the ice.... The bleeping guys couldn't clear the bleeping puck.... (Pierre) Turgeon was flailing away at the bleeping thing but couldn't get it out to save his bleeping life…"

On and on he went for a long half-minute, with the spit flying and the veins bulging in his neck. Who could blame Quenneville for feeling a little pressure, what with the difficulties faced by his injury-plagued roster, and his own perceived coaching shortcomings at the end of a tough hockey game? Coach "Q" had to be hoping that his team could get healthy, mentally at least, against the Wild, but the Blues were to receive no cooperation from the home team on this March evening.

Despite the strong performance against the Blues, the Wild men were still fighting a tough battle. A 6-2 thumping at the hands of O'Donnell's new team, the Devils, at Continental Airlines Arena, came even though the Wild outshot the home team 28-27 in the loss. The Wild garnered a win the next night, 4-1 over the New York Islanders in New York, giving a victory to goalie Derek Gustafson in his NHL debut. They were leading the Isles 4-0 before a late goal with less than two minutes remaining spoiled Gustafson's bid for an inaugural shutout. Although the Islanders struggled all year, finishing with the worst record in hockey, it was nice to see the Minnesotans put the hammer down on a team they could handle.

"We don't throw any wins back," said Jacques Lemaire.

The Wild played what arguably were two of their best games of the year when they returned home for contests with the Detroit Red Wings on a Sunday evening and St Louis again the following Wednesday. Although both games resulted in overtime losses for the Wild, they played some great hockey and felt they should have come out with more than two points for their efforts.

It would be a battle night-in and night-out for the Wild for the rest of the year, and the way they played against Detroit showed that the players understood that fact. The Red Wings would defeat the Wild 3-2 in overtime on Brendan Shanahan's game winner just 37 seconds into overtime, and outshoot the home team 38-22, but it was a battle to be savored by the 18,568 in attendance. The boys played their hearts out, and Jacques said he was as proud of their effort as any all season. Manny Fernandez was absolutely stellar between the pipes, with two Detroit goals coming on well-executed power plays by the Wings and no fault of Manny's.

After Detroit's victory, the man who scored the game winner, Shanahan, took notice of the Wild's great effort. "They have such a difficult style to play against when they get the lead," said the Red Wing's regular-season top scorer. "We battled back and told ouselves we needed to remain patient, because they can frustrate you with their work ethic."

The Wild were outshot 15-5 in the second period after taking a 2-0 lead on goals by Darby Hendrickson, who opened the scoring seven minutes into the first, and Sergei Krivokrasov early in the second. It was during the second session that Detroit began playing with a fury that would not be denied on this night; the Wings had already lost the first two games against the Wild, and were determined to gain a victory this time. But that was the awesome thing about the game, as well as the 1-0 loss to St.

Louis a few days later (an equally tough battle). These playoff-tested veteran teams were having to fight for their lives to squeak out a victory over the newcomers, leaving it all on the ice to garner an overtime win. In fact, the Wild were outplaying the Blues before Scott Young's shot from beyond the blue line squeezed past a screened Jamie McLennan in the extra session, a tough break for the home team.

The boys were rightfully proud of their efforts against the Wings and the Blues; team Captain Darby Hendrickson said, "despite the loss (to St. Louis), I feel that was one of the best games we played all year. The hustle was there all night, we were working all shifts and we just needed a break to finish it off. It was a tough loss, but also heartening in how we played." The Wild outshot the Blues 21-15 and dominated the third period, holding St. Louis to just one shot on goal over the 20 minutes.

The Wild followed their strong play at home against the two powers with an uninspired performance in Philadelphia. The "Broad Street Bullies" pounded the Wild as Flyers All-Star goalie Roman Cechmanek stopped all 15 shots he faced in a 3-0 win. It was a bad loss for the Wild, and a disappointed Darby Hendrickson stated, "We were flat. I don't know what it was, but we didn't play our brand of hockey." It was a defeat made worse by the ankle injury suffered by Manny Fernandez midway through the second period, which turned out to be a season-ending injury for the Wild's number-one goalie.

The Wild suffered their fourth straight defeat three nights later at Colorado. Minnesota came out flying and opened up a two-goal lead on goals from the "Trencin Connection," Marian Gaborik and Lubomir Sekeras. Milan Hejduk scored to make it 2-1, with Hendrickson again creating a two-goal cushion on his 14th goal of the season. It wouldn't hold, as Colorado came back with three unanswered goals from Martin Skoula, Hejduk and Joe Sakic. Sakic's clincher came against Wild goalie Jamie McLennan with 1:47 remaining. Minnesota had played a strong game, but was not strong enough to defeat the powerful Avalanche.

Returning home, the Wild dropped their fifth straight game, 4-1, to the Dallas Stars. Mike Modano started fast for Dallas, scoring the first two goals of the game. Following a scoreless second period, Antti Laaksonen put the Wild on the board early in the third, a short-handed goal from a nice feed by Wes Walz, to cut the lead in half. The home team outshot the visitors in both the second and third periods, but John Maclean scored at 16:24 of the third and Shaun Van Allen iced the game with a shorthanded goal.

Hendrickson felt good about the effort sustained by the Wild. "We kept working and never gave up despite falling behind early on the Modano goals. That's what we have to do, and I thought we might go over the top after Antti's goal. It didn't happen, but that's the way we've got to play. We have to keep pushing."

The Wild were looking to bust loose, but the Nashville Predators, in town March 21, were a tough team to get healthy against offensively. Nashville had great goaltending that had kept them in hockey games all year. Mike Dunham played with determination and skill, and the Predators had a lot of young players on their roster. Marian Cisar, Scott Hartnell (still a teenager), Denis Arkipov and David Legwand were already good, and they're going to get better with experience.

The Predators had allowed fewer than 20 shots in four of their last six games coming in. The Wild's power play efforts remained frustrating, with the rate of success now under 10% for the year. They were last in the league in the category, and desperately needed to show some offense. They had won only three of their last eighteen and wanted to make a strong showing, and get the win, against Nashville.

Minnesota came out with guns blazing. They applied constant pressure on Dunham, outshooting the Predators 12-3 in the first period and dominating the action. The fans were roaring in a display that was typical of the support the Wild had enjoyed all year. It was to no avail, however. Dunham made the big saves, including a gem on Marian Gaborik from point-blank range, and the two teams played to a scoreless tie. It was the second 0-0 game of the season, the first having been against Florida in October. Jamie McLennan must be one of the very few goalies in NHL history to post shutouts on two occasions and not get the win in either one.

Nashville outshot the Wild 24-11 after the first period, outshooting them 27-23 for the game. Minnesota again failed to take advantage of some early opportunities and appeared tired late in the game. Following the contest, Jacques Lemaire commented that "With McLennan in goal, we're just not scoring as much. He played very well tonight, but we're not finishing."

The Wild dropped another tough one to Detroit in the Motor City. Darby Hendrickson gave Minnesota a 2-1 lead at 4:21 of the second period, but the Red Wings rebounded with three unanswered goals to seal a 4-2 victory. "When we had the lead, I felt we were going to maintain it," said Hendrickson. "They turned it up a notch and we didn't respond as well as we're capable of."

Back home to play Vancouver, the Wild fought back from a 2-0 deficit to gain yet another tie, this one 2-2. There was some satisfaction in the minds of the players, in that they had gained a point against the tough Canucks, but Jacques' post–game comments were not all positive. "I didn't appreciate the first period at all. Our minds weren't there; I didn't think we were sharp at all. When you want to make five passes before getting out of your zone, it's not gonna work.

"The second goal (by Filip Kuba) gave us a real lift. He's playing very well for us. I would have to say I'm surprised at how far he has come and how good a player he has been."

Hendrickson was thinking after the game that he would like to have scored the winning goal in overtime against his former team. He worked hard in the extra session, but it was not to be. "If I'd scored the winning goal, I might've skated by the (Vancouver) bench," he said as he pulled off the sweater with the big "C" on the shoulder. "Nothing too major, no big celebration." He sighed, and added, "It would've been nice, but it didn't happen."

Yes, it would've been nice. Captain Darby Hendrickson skating by the bench of the Vancouver team that didn't protect him in the expansion draft.

THIRTEEN

WILD BEHAVIOR
It's a Jungle on the Ice

Most hockey fans are familiar with the Marty McSorley slash on Donald Brashear in Vancouver on February 21, 2000. McSorley was playing for the Boston Bruins, who had signed him as a free agent in December of 1999, when he stick-assaulted the Canuck's Brashear in Vancouver, a move that nearly cost Brashear the sight in one eye and brought stiff repercussions from the league and from the authorities, including a criminal trial in British Columbia. There is a theory expounded by hockey people that McSorley was looking for a fight with Brashear to avenge an earlier loss in a bout with the burly Canuck. Brashear was not responding to the unwritten tough-guy code that requires the victor to offer a rematch to the vanquished, so McSorley, the thinking goes, was trying to instigate a fight and didn't really mean to hurt him with his stick.

This falls in with the thinking that Toronto's Tie Domi was really just going for the shoulder, not the head, of New Jersey's Scott Niedermayer with his vicious elbow in game six of the 2000 Eastern Conference finals. Either way, this kind of play is idiocy and has big consequences for both the offending and the offended parties. The slash resulted in the sad finale of a rocking hockey career for Marty McSorley, and the ironic result of Domi's blow was the dispiriting and tremendous weakening of a seemingly in-control Maple Leaf team trying for its first Stanley Cup appearance in 34 years.

It was of interest to some that Marty McSorley was trying to get his career back on track in early February of 2001 by joining the Grand Rapids Griffins of the IHL. The 17-year NHL veteran, who had won Stanley Cups with Wayne Gretzky and the Edmonton Oilers in 1987 and 1988, played his first game with the Griffins on the same day he had signed a contract with the team.

Lo and behold, with just under 18 minutes left in a game with the Utah Grizzlies, and the Griffins leading 2-0, McSorley jumped into a fracas involving several players from both teams. The man who spent 3,381 minutes in the penalty box during his NHL career, and had one season with 399 minutes (Los Angeles Kings, 1992-93) was hit with a five minute penalty for fighting and a game misconduct penalty.

Speaking after the 3-1 Grand Rapids victory, McSorley said he jumped into the brawl when he saw two Utah players pounding one of his new teammates. It was too much for the old gladiator to take, and he flew into the fight with both fists blazing. He said he had no regrets about being ejected for fighting in his comeback game. "If the same thing were to happen again, then I'm going to get involved again," the Hamilton, Ontario native said. "But I'm not here looking for fights."

McSorley is kind of like the old gunfighter who will never outlive his reputation. The big defenseman, who ranks third in the NHL in career penalty minutes, had tangled earlier in the game with a Grizzlies left wing who had sought him out. McSorley is trying to make it back to the NHL, and there's not much use in trying to teach this old dog any new tricks. Although he had several productive offensive seasons for the Kings, accumulating around 40 points during each of a few consecutive years, Marty McSorley will be remembered as the roughest of heavyweights—who made a serious mistake.

There is a whole lot of hacking going on in the National Hockey League. The league has been trying for years to get on top of it, but one has to wonder if it really wants to. We are, after all, a society tuned into the "sport" of professional wrestling, which isn't wrestling at all. We know that violence sells from watching the evening news, yet the slashing and hacking that is such a challenge for the league to control is simply not a necessary part of the sport.

Enforcers play a role in the game; they help to keep the guys who fly around the ice on offense healthy. Marty McSorley, who made a living protecting Wayne Gretzky, made an interesting point in a conversation a few years ago with the *Los Angeles Daily News.* "Your real tough guys don't bother your goal scorers. The tough guys monitor the goal scorers and the tough guys get rid of the gnats—get rid of the annoying guys who slow the game down."

McSorley didn't get in trouble with Donald Brashear because he beat him up. His career was damaged due to the fact that he used his stick as a weapon. A key point to be made is that the human fist is significantly less dangerous a weapon than a hockey stick swung with near-lethal force.

"I don't mind the players who have a role to protect their top guys," said Jacques Lemaire. "But all the stuff with the sticks serves no purpose except to injure and fill the penalty box."

The heavy wielding of sticks has become a way of checking an opponent, with the whacking of legs, arms and occasionally the head and neck, having become a part of doing business. No one is immune, as countless players have lost time due to injuries inflicted by this misuse of a stick, to the detriment of their team's ability to compete. When Mario Lemieux had his hand broken by an Adam Graves slash during the '92 playoffs, it altered the course of the Stanley Cup playoffs. Who knows how that injury affected the defending Cup champions, who lost the best player in the game at crunch time?

Players are bigger and stronger today than ever before, but the ice surface is still 200 feet by 85 feet. Injuries are a part of the game, but more and more players are being sidelined by injuries that should be avoidable. Players are taking shortcuts to find a path to victory, and in the process they're causing damage to the sport.

When a team's best players are forced off the ice, everyone suffers: the fans who buy the tickets and fill the seats, the owners who pay the salaries, and the players themselves. All are hurt when key guys go on the injured list. Hockey players may feel they are indestructable, but of course they are not. Any one guy is capable of damaging another's career. It's a given that a number of the league's elite players face the possibility of being singled out, and taken out of games by means other than clean play.

Big hits on the ice are expected. Physical play is what the NHL is all about, but all agree that random use of the stick as a weapon has no place in hockey today. Deliberate intent to injure must be dealt with severely. That is where the head of officials, Andy van Hellemond, is trying to come to the rescue. He needs to back up his words of "zero tolerance" with action, and things are slowly moving in the right direction. Van Hellemond, a no-nonsense official long respected by most in the game, has his work cut out for him.

Jacques Lemaire is admittedly no fan of the slash, hook or hack. He is of the opinion that referees miss a lot of the flagrant action that takes place on the ice. He would usually express his displeasure with the officials' blind spots quietly, asking questions that would indicate he didn't agree with a call, and in a non-confrontational manner make his point.

Things changed after the Detroit game on March 11, which resulted in a Wild loss in overtime. Curtis Leschyshyn was called for a questionable interference penalty with the game tied and 45 seconds remaining in the third period. That call resulted in a Detroit power play extending into the overtime; Brendan Shanahan's game-winning score came just 37 seconds in.

It was a tough loss to swallow. The Wild had fought valiantly and felt they deserved a better fate than to have a potential win snatched from their grasp by a referee, Brad Meier, who had been a festering thorn in their side.

Following the game, Jacques Lemaire stated publicly that Meier had told him at the Vancouver game a week before that "he was going to get back at me" for having complained about calls (in the Edmonton game on March 2). Lemaire had been increasingly unhappy with Meier since a 4-1 loss at Colorado on February 23, when Meier gave goalie Jamie McLennan an unsportsmanlike conduct penalty for griping about the fact that Meier didn't check the video replay on a contested goal.

In the Edmonton game, where the Wild extended their winless streak to six games, McLennan stopped 26 of 29 shots, but apparently not a key goal when it looked like he had possession of a loose puck in the crease. It was the same type of non-call that had occurred in Colorado.

"There's no doubt I had control of the puck," said McLennan after the loss. "There was a lot of whacking at it and when I heard the whistle, I moved away. They said it was a goal, but no way was that a goal.

"I think the referee (Meier) was looking for his whistle. The whistle was late, but that doesn't matter because the puck didn't cross the line until after the whistle blew. I asked for a replay, and he gave it to me this time." A replay was granted but provided no insight.

Then, with 3:20 left in the hockey game, Meier steamed the Wild again. Moments before Edmonton's Rem Murray put the game away with his second goal of the evening, Stacy Roest was pulled down to the ice in full view of the the officials. Again, there was no whistle. Edmonton scored and the Wild staff took a two-minute bench penalty as the Wild went on to lose 3-1 to the Oilers.

Things apparently got worse in Vancouver a couple of nights later during a 4-3 Minnesota overtime victory. That was the night that Lemaire believes that Meier made the statement about "getting back at me" for his grumbling in Edmonton. Then came the Detroit game, and Brendan Shanahan's game-ending power play goal.

Lemaire's frustration originated from the fact that he believed Meier was out of position and unable to see the puck on numerous occasions, costing his team at critical junctures. There was also a feeling that the Wild were suffering a lack of respect from the officials, perhaps deriving from their expansion team status.

Asked later about his observations on Mr. Meier's fairness and competency, which ended up drawing a good deal of media attention and costing him $5,000, Jacques seemed in good humor. "The refs can be lousy, but the league still needs to stand up for its officials. It does no good to talk about it, but I can tell you this. I don't care what the referees think of me, some of them need to do a better job. That includes more than just one.

"I think it's a little bit like the way the police are; they can be wrong, but they are still the police," said a smiling, though clearly annoyed, coach Lemaire.

So how could they do a better job, he was asked?

"We would be better off if the referees were outside the ice surface."

I figured Lemaire was pulling my leg and told him so.

"I'm serious," he said. "They could be stationed behind the net, because there is a lot of stuff that is going on that they don't see. The referee could see a lot more if he did not have to skate, did not have to avoid a hit or avoid the puck. If he was watching and studying the game, he would see more than when he is on the ice.

"The coaches are a good example," Lemaire continued. "You think we are always watching the game, but we are always missing things (from) behind the bench. Coaches are making the line changes or looking to see if someone is hurt, always something. We are trying to watch the game all the time, but at the same time we're not. There's a line change and we are looking away and suddenly there's a goal or there's a slash and we didn't see it. If we were only watching the game we would see a lot more."

Jacques is calm and collected when he is discussing the officiating. He smiles when I give him a funny look regarding off-ice refereeing, and cites another example to support his thinking. "Mike Ramsey confirmed my feelings on this when I put him in charge of the defensemen. He was responsible for changing the defensemen, watching the play and correcting certain things. Mike said to me, 'This is unreal. When I'm changing the guys—and there's just six of them—I don't see half the game.'

"There's no doubt about all the aggravation they (the referees) go through with the coaches and the players, and it's a distraction. It has to be. After every call, somebody is going to get on them. I really feel that they would do a better job if they were not on the ice.

"Besides, it's human nature to have problems with certain people at certain times. We're all human beings and sometimes we get upset. Officials are no different from anybody else. Just like a policeman, you may not like his style and he may not like the way you are looking at him.

"But he's in control, he's in charge. That's how it is."

It's interesting to hear this poised and dignified man wrestle with the question of officiating—just like the coaches of all teams in all sports. It reminded me of something that Glen Sonmor, no stranger to strong debate with referees, said to me regarding hockey officials: "I think that I shall never see, a satisfactory ref-er-ee," quoth Sonmor. "But you know, all in all I think they do a pretty good job. Or, as (former Boston GM) Lynn Patrick used to say, 'It's amazing how well-officiated the games are that I'm not involved in.'

"There's a lot of truth to that."

I don't think Jacques Lemaire was entirely serious when he made his post-game comments about Brad Meier. Yes, the words came out as reported, but they were spoken matter-of-factly; he's not a man who ordinarily holds grudges about such things as bad calls. Jacques clearly believes that referees do miss calls, some more than others, but his anger was made large by the cumulative effect that Meier's calls were having on his team.

Several Wild players felt that Jacques was indeed standing up for them with his vocal protests. Wes Walz, for one, said, "It meant something to the players that Jacques stood up for us. It shows how much he cares about the guys and that he's willing to fight for us."

Jacques Lemaire was angry with what he considered very poor officiating, and while he no doubt did hear something from Meier that he felt was out of line, it was most important that he make a clear stand for his men. More important than any particular play, he wanted McLennan, Walz and the rest of the team to know that he was behind them all the way.

FOURTEEN

A WILD SEASON WINDS DOWN

By the end of March, the Minnesota Wild season was a guaranteed record-breaking success at the gate. On March 28, when the Phoenix Coyotes came to town, the Wild established an NHL expansion-team attendance record at Xcel Energy Center, totaling 717,336 fans for the season—with two home games remaining. The Wild had averaged 18,393 fans per home date thus far, more than 300 over the stadium's stated capacity of 18,064.

But the game against the Coyotes was another tough battle on the ice. The Wild seemed to outskate and outhustle the playoff-hunting Coyotes, but to no avail. Despite outshooting the visitors 29-19, the Wild dropped the contest 2-0. It was another tough loss and extended the club's winless streak to nine games. Still, Jacques Lemaire praised his club in the postgame media conference. "I can't ask for more from the guys when they work that hard. I know they're doing the best they can, and that's all a coach can hope for," said Lemaire. "We're still struggling to put the puck in the net."

Shane Doan scored for the Coyotes just 0:36 into the game, the fastest goal ever allowed by the Wild at the start of a contest. The quick goal seemed to ignite the home team, as Minnesota outshot the Coyotes 15-7 in the first period and kept intense pressure on Phoenix goalie Sean Burke the rest of the evening. Burke was up to it, however, gaining his 4th shutout of the year in an exceptional performance.

Doan's second goal of the evening and 25th of the season, which came on the Coyote's first shot of the 3rd period with just under nine minutes left, beat goalie Derek Gustafson after yet another Wild flurry had failed to pot the puck. That finished off the Wild's hopes to stop a winless streak at eight games. The Minnesota squad was now in the midst of a nine-game drought, with tough games coming up on the road with San Jose and Edmonton before the closing home stand with the rival Columbus Blue Jackets and President's Trophy-clinching Colorado Avalanche. There was to be no rest for the wounded.

By late March, the Wild had gone through a tough stretch, going winless in their last nine games. Despite a number of tough battles that included a couple of ties and overtime losses, the Wild had not won in almost three weeks. Lemaire was asked if it frustrated him to be missing some of the key players who had departed through trades (Scott Pellerin, Sean O'Donnell, and Curtis Leschyshyn). It would be only natural to feel some frustration, right?

Not right. He leaned back in his chair and glanced at the small chalk board on his wall. "No, it really doesn't bother me. I'm not frustrated that those guys are gone. We are on the right track and that's what's important here, even though we haven't won in the last nine games or something."

I was a little surprised that he knew how long the team had gone winless. Perhaps he had read the paper or seen it on TV, things he would not have done when he grew tired of the media in New Jersey and Montreal. He had even had a famous battle with one particular writer for the New York Post, and had refused post-game interviews for a time. That has not happened in the Twin Cities, where he has a good working relationship with the journalists closest to the team.

The Wild had lost to Phoenix 2-0 the night before in a typically hard-fought contest. It was a game that they could have won, against a playoff-contending team, if only they could have put the puck in the net when the opportunities presented themselves. But Lemaire was good-humored, smiling easily as he discussed details of the game. He seemed genuinely pleased with the effort and said he felt good about his squad.

"The guys are fighting. We've had a few ties during this stretch, and we have been in every game except maybe one. We were close in almost all of them. For a first-year team I think we are doing pretty well, despite the fact we have a goaltender and a few other guys injured, plus three of our better players gone from the team. And still the guys compete with all they've got. So I'm very happy with that."

The coach leaned forward over his desk and paused, smiling again. "How can I not be? They've done everything I asked them to do."

Lemaire then took a moment to look toward the future.

"I don't think Doug wants to make a lot of changes, but he wants to make changes that will bring the team to another level. We want to move up, we want to move forward. We were looking at the (N.Y.) Islanders this morning. We were looking at their last several drafts and the players that they drafted. Among the players drafted high, a very large number of them are still in the league and they're pretty good players. The

Islanders might have had a pretty good team if they had held on to them, but now they have the worst record. We know we have to be careful with every move we make if we want to keep moving up. You don't want to get rid of guys just to make a move, just to do something."

So what has to happen to make a brand new hockey team successful?

Lemaire reflected for a moment and said, "I think you need to have confidence that you will succeed and get the players to where they feel good about themselves. Great teams have a belief that it's their year, that it's their season. Good things start to happen when you believe. It's an attitude thing and we had a little bit of this happening during our season. When we had the toughest month of the season, the guys played very well against the top teams."

He was referring to the run of games, from Los Angeles on December 2 through Detroit on January 5, in which the Wild never lost by more than a goal and had an undefeated streak of eight games. Lemaire laughed as I recited the games making up the streak: Dallas, a 6-0 hammering; Ottawa, a 2-2 tie; Los Angeles, a 4-3 win; a 5-3 victory at Detroit, ties with Phoenix and Atlanta sandwiched around a win over Anaheim; and finally, another victory (3-2) over Detroit at home.

"We were on a run there and a lot of things were going well for us. Nothing seemed to be bothering the guys and they came to play every game. We did well there for a while," he said, his voice tapering off. "We did well."

There was clearly a quiet satisfaction in the memory of games well played.

"This year there is not a single bad attitude on the team. Not this year," he repeated, knowing that there may have been times in his coaching past when there was a problem or two, but not with this group. "This year every player that we've had here has been listening and doing the things that we have asked of them. They wanted a position on this club. The players wanted a job and they've all worked to keep their job."

Lemaire truly respects his players. For what they have accomplished, and who they have become. He doesn't always show it, but there's no question he has genuine affection for the men who were a part of the Wild's first season. There's going to be a different feel going forward, and there has to be growth.

"Next year might be a little tougher for some of the guys," Lemaire said quietly. "We are going to demand a little more, and some of the guys will be able to give a little more and some will not be able to. It will be a little tougher. We do have to move on and improve as a club, and we are going to try and take the right way to get there. It's a matter of learning. There's nothing for me to say if someone makes a mistake. Everyone makes mistakes, but you have to learn from your mistakes to get better.

"It's like the goaltenders. I tell them to watch the tapes of their games, to see how a goal came in, to see how they made the stops. 'What is your position when the player is behind you? When you get a shot from the side? When the play is in front of you? How did the puck get in? And what can you do differently, if anything?' That's how you learn.

"But if you can't look at that and you just play the same game, you'll never get better than you are right now. And it is that way for every player. Some players, when they look at the videotape, see the mistake and they feel embarrassed. They know they made a mistake, but they're not thinking about the changes that they need to make the next time. So I will try to explain things to them. And they have to listen so that the next time, when the same situation arises, they will respond differently. All players, even the best ones, can get better."

I reminded Lemaire of a conversation we'd had earlier in the year, when the question was posed as to how many games the Wild might win. The number 25 was thrown out for consideration, and he had laughed when he said, "I'll take that!" Now, the team was headed for close to that number of victories, despite a tough stretch. Are you okay with that, Jacques?

"It's not bad. This has been a great year, a special year. I don't want it to end. But we have to keep getting better."

FIFTEEN

WILD TIMES AHEAD

The Scouts Take on the Draft

The Minnesota Wild respect the New Jersey Devils model of building a team in large part through the entry draft. A look at the Devils roster reveals that Devils GM Lou Lamoriello has constructed his team by drafting wisely, making shrewd trades and acquiring good, cost-effective free agents. The result has been Stanley Cup Championships in 1995 and 2000, with another finals appearance in 2001. Doug Risebrough notes the approximately $25 million payroll difference in 2001 between the Stanley Cup finalist Devils and the champion Colorado Avalanche. "There are different ways to get to where you want to go in this game, and I think we're closer to the New Jersey model than the Colorado model," Risebrough said. "I think New Jersey has recognized the importance of developing players for the long term, and we're going to take the same course."

To that end, the Wild have scouts all over the globe, including recent additions to the team's scouting staff in Russia, Slovakia, and the Czech Republic, as well as two more in North America. There are now 20 scouts working in Minnesota's scouting department on a full- or part-time basis. Tommy Thompson and Guy Lapointe head up the Wild's scouting department and direct the Club's pre-draft activities. Chief amateur scout Thompson was optimistic about the 2001 entry draft, noting that the Wild would get five picks in the first 103 selections. "There's a lot of talent this year, and with a number of early picks, we have a good chance to find some solid prospects," Thompson said.

Minnesota Wild chief amateur scout Tommy Thompson goes on the road to see about 200 hockey games a year. He's a scholarly looking man with a great sense of humor who happens to hold a law degree. Thompson also has a passion for the game of baseball. In fact, he used to coach Minnesota Twins third baseman Corey Koskie as a young ballplayer up in Canada. Koskie was a goalie when he was growing up in Manitoba, though Thompson said, "I think he made the right decision to stick with baseball."

Thompson acknowledges the very demanding nature of the business of scouting. It's hard to avoid the rigors of the road when that's where you spend more than half your life; hanging out in airports and hotels, trying to eat properly in foreign lands while waiting for games, and enduring the general wear and tear of extensive travel. Part of the compensation is the camaraderie found among brothers in the game. "There's a bond in scouting, and it's a lot of fun going to the rink for games and discussing hockey with your peers," according to Thompson.

Different scouts may have different priorities, but they all are ultimately looking for two things: character and talent. Wild scout Glen Sonmor likes to look at a prospect's overall athleticism. "I'm a big fan of athletes," Sonmor said, "not just hockey players. I'm looking for athletic intelligence as well as hockey sense."

Sonmor is known to watch a prospect play in a variety of other sports to get a better read on athletic potential. Paul Martin of Elk River, Minnesota and the University of Minnesota, now in the New Jersey Devils system, was watched from the stands by Sonmor as he played point guard in high school basketball and set school records for receptions as a football wide receiver. "You learn a lot from the way they compete in other sports. I'm a believer that, if an athlete is so inclined, there are benefits to playing a variety of sports as a youth."

There was one player in the 2001 draft who is expected to make an immediate impact when he joins the NHL. Ilya Kovalchuk is a big, smooth-skating right wing with a reputation for toughness. "He's gotten a lot of publicity, and he warrants it," said Thompson. "Kovalchuk's a spectacular-looking player, 6' 2" and about 220 when I saw him—a little overweight, perhaps; I think he should play around 210. He can skate, he's dynamic and he's a very exciting player; there's no question about that. And probably, given his physical attributes, he's more ready to play than anyone in the draft." The Atlanta Flames, who took Kovalchuk with the number one pick, will find out whether he will be a Mario Lemieux (first pick, 1984), a Mike Modano (1988) or something of a lesser light.

The Wild finished out of the running for the lone help-you-right-away prospect in the draft. Without getting into the details of the NHL's formula for determining the order in which teams pick, suffice it to say that, in general, the worse a team's record is, the better its chances of getting the number-one pick. Wild scout Sonmor laughed as he recalled how his old boss, Lou Nanne, might have played Doug Risebrough's GM role. "I think Louie might have had the 3rd goalie in there late in the season, trying for one of those top picks," Sonmor said with a smile. "To get that first pick, he might have wanted to try that fellow who's had the hot hand at Guelph, Ontario, in the Ontario Hockey League. Or perhaps the 'top gun' at Chicoutimi. He might say, 'Let's bring him up and take a good look at him at this level. Maybe he'll surprise us.'" Sonmor was kidding and laughed at the thought. "The players and the coaches won't slow down a bit, because all they want to do is win. Sometimes it can be a little tough for the guys planning the future of the team; they want the best prospect. This year you have a situation where the top amateur player eligible for the entry draft looks to be head and shoulders above the rest, and drafting Kovalchuk is not going to happen for the Wild this year."

Thompson acknowledged that selecting the top hockey players in the first round of an NHL entry draft is not an exact science. First round draft picks who don't make it to the NHL are usually misjudged on attributes other than their ability to play hockey. "It comes down to character, and the personal skills a player has available to make the adjustment to professional hockey. It's like hiring someone for a business. Once you do, they have to want to make their work a success."

Thompson noted that the talent pool in hockey is growing and has spread throughout the world. "The player base is broader than it has ever been. There are players with a wide variety of backgrounds, from high school and college hockey, as well as the Europeans now. I think I was scouting in the league for 15 years before I ever heard of a Slovakian player, but you had better be over there now.

"It's a competitive business, and it's important to get the correct read on a player. A scout has to watch out for red flags that might emerge, and we utilize an interview process to help weed out players who, for example, are unwilling to make the necessary commitment at a young age. Remember, these are 18- and 19-year-old players and you really have to go with a gut feeling, but you try to back up that feeling as much as possible."

The Wild philosophy is to take the proverbial "best player available" in all rounds of the selection process. It's a policy endorsed by former Mighty Ducks GM Jack Ferreira, who said before the draft that "you need to take the best player available at the time you select, because by the time he is ready for the NHL, your needs have probably changed."

"We don't have enough depth anywhere that we can be trying to fill particular holes," said Tommy Thompson. "We're pleased with the progress of some of our young people, but it's not like we're going to say, 'forget defensemen now, we've got enough.' We do need the best hockey players we can get. We're looking for athletes who have the attributes to play the type of hockey the Minnesota Wild plays—the up-tempo, fast-paced hockey that you saw the Wild play in their first year—and we hope to find a bunch of them."

Strong, athletic hockey players were on the Wild menu at the National Car Center in Florida, home of the Florida Panthers, in late June of 2001. With the sixth pick of the first round they selected a player who possesses the tools, albeit unrefined, that the Wild keenly desire. They took Mikko Koivu, an 18-year-old center from Turku, Finland with size (6' 2", 185 pounds) and speed that Tommy Thompson and Guy Lapointe couldn't resist. He's the younger brother of Montreal Canadiens captain Saku Koivu, and has the potential to be the kind of set-up man that the Wild sorely need on the power play.

A close-up look at Mikko after the selection revealed a young man with a lot of poise and the look of a competitor. He seemed to exhibit a maturity that belied his years as he easily responded to reporters' questions. He gives a firm handshake, and speaks of the "normal youth" his family life offered. "My father made sure that we stayed focused on school and family things," said the soft-spoken Finn. This helped to explain a perception that his father had kept him off-limits from the press, with one scribe informing me that "we tried to talk to him, but we could never track the kid down. It was frustrating, it was like he didn't exist." Perhaps that is understandable, given the father's familiarity with the draft process through his experience with Saku (Montreal's 21st pick of the first round in 1993).

The Wild felt strongly about Mikko Koivu, and the blood line is outstanding. His brother tied for the lead in scoring with the Canadiens in 2000-2001 (17 goals, 30 assists, 47 points), but will be away from hockey for the foreseeable future as he battles cancer. While Saku knows his brother needs seasoning, he likes his little brother's chances. "Mikko played for the same TPS Turku team that I did. Half the time he played with the junior club and half the time with the Division 1 team. He's playing in a lot of games and getting much-needed experience."

The Wild will not rush the young Finn to the NHL. They are excited, however, and confident that Mikko's style of play, very much like his brother's, will make him an excellent playmaker. His overall skill level is extremely high, and a bonus is that "he's much bigger than his brother," said Goran Stubb of the European Scouting Service. He's bigger now, largely due to a growth spurt during the last year, according to Tommy Thompson. "A year ago he was a tall, gangly kid who looked a little stiff out on the ice. But he had some tools, and now he looks much better athletically. He's a very smart player who is highly skilled with the puck. He's still wiry, but he's going to fill out and be a big, strong center one of these days."

Thompson likes to say that developing a hockey player is a little like baking a cake. You mix in all the ingredients, and put it in the oven. Now, some cakes may take a little longer to cook than other cakes, but the length of cooking doesn't hurt the flavor of the finished product. Tommy looks at hockey players that way; he thinks it's safe to say that Mikko Koivu may not see the inside of the Xcel Energy Center for a couple of years, but when he does he's going to be one heck of a player. "The kid has a tremendous upside," Thompson said.

The Minnesota Wild continue to put together the best possible group of players they can to be competitive in the NHL. The entry draft is a big part of that program. But, as Jacques Lemaire noted at the end of the first season, on his way to a luncheon and then the airport for his summer break, there's a tough road to the playoffs. "Look at the teams who didn't make the playoffs this year, some of the teams who were supposed to. Like Phoenix, Boston, Edmonton, and Nashville; those are all good hockey teams. They're going to want to be in the playoffs next year, and maybe a couple more teams will emerge. We need to build our hockey team, and developing players is important. Nashville is a good hockey team, and a very young hockey team. We want to be like them, pushing for the playoffs."

The Draft: A Case Study

Ontario Hockey League center Jason Spezza provides an interesting study of the way NHL scouts think. Over the course of the draft week, it became clear that Spezza's stock had fallen dramatically. He had been seen as a potential first pick a few months earlier, but now he was projected to slide as far as the fifth pick by one GM. Why? What had young Mr. Spezza done to precipitate such a drop?

"After watching him over the course of the year, it's become apparent that he's not the skater he was cracked up to be," a Calgary scout said about Spezza. "Also, his attitude could be better." An employee of NHL Central Scouting reported, "It's like he's been paying attention to the media reports placing him in the top two in the draft, and he's not playing as hard any more. I watched one of his games and he was practically invisible in the third period."

At lunch in the dining room of the media hotel I ran into Mike Kelly, President of the Windsor Spitfires, the team for which Spezza plays. He sounded frustrated by the perception that Spezza is anything but a solid, hard-working, very exceptional player. "He's a great, great player and he's going to have an excellent NHL career. There's no doubt in my mind about that. You have to like the way he thinks on the ice; he tends to make good decisions and has the 'fast hands' that make him a strong passer and shooter."

There are those who believe a conspiracy theory is in order: Perhaps a few teams are putting out the word on Spezza, hoping that he'll fall to their position in the draft. If he does, Kelly is convinced that they'll get a gem. "We know that Ilya (Kovalchuk, the number one pick of the draft by the Atlanta Flames) has had his stock increase of late, but I don't believe that should reflect on Jason. He still may be the best player over the long term."

Kelly was soon to be vindicated, with the Ottawa Senators and New York Islanders making a big trade just prior to the selection process. About one hour before the draft, word spread that the Senators had sent Alexei Yashin to the Isles for the second pick in the draft. They then used the pick to take Spezza, about whom Ottawa GM Marshall Johnson was excited but realistic. "We feel we picked up a very strong player who will help us, whose potential is very good. We have to understand that he's just 18 years old, and we have to understand that we are giving up a 40-goal star for someone who hasn't played a game in the NHL, but that's all part of what's going on."

The move is a risky one for Islander GM Mike Milbury. Yashin had sat out a season to protest his contract with Ottawa and had a reputation, in some circles, for being a difficult player. When asked if there was a "fear factor" in trading for him, Milbury responded that he didn't think so. "I haven't spoken to Alexei yet, but I think he's probably learned some valuable lessons. He clearly will make our power players much better. I'm looking forward to sitting down with him and getting a contract done as soon as possible." Milbury paused and added, "Well, I lied to you about that. I'm not looking forward to it at all." He shouldn't have been, as it cost the Islanders $87 million to sign Yashin for 10 years. Time will determine whether the move for Yashin was wise.

WRAPPING
IT UP

The Wild tied the Edmonton Oilers at Skyreach Centre 2-2 in their final road game of their first season. Stacy Roest opened the scoring for the Wild with a power play goal at 1:43 of the first period, and Pavel Patera added a goal in the second period to give the Wild a 2-1 lead. It looked like the Wild would gain their first victory in over three weeks, but the Oilers Doug Weight scored with 0:48 left in the contest to force a 2-2 tie. That was how it ended following a scoreless overtime.

Despite the tie, Wild GM Doug Risebrough felt the club had given one of its gutsiest performances of the season. "That was a game where I was extremely proud of our guys. They were really beat at the end of a tough road trip, a difficult stretch in general, and they really fought hard. It's a game I'll remember not for the final score, certainly, but for what I saw from our players. They just wouldn't quit."

Two nights later, against the Columbus Blue Jackets at the "X," Darby Hendrickson's second goal of the game, with 1:20 remaining, gave Minnesota an exciting and hard-fought 3-2 victory. Wes Walz scored the other goal for the Wild, giving both Hendrickson and Walz 17 for the season. The Wild were not to be denied this night, out-shooting the Blue Jackets 32-19 in garnering the club's first win since March 9th.

The Wild closed the season on a Sunday afternoon against the Colorado Avalanche. Joe Sakic showed the Xcel Energy Center crowd why he is one of the best in the game by scoring two goals as the Avs defeated the home team 4-2 in the finale. Colorado took a 3-0 lead with just over 12 minutes to go in the second period, but Minnesota rushed back into the contest behind scores by Walz, his seventh shorthanded goal of the year, and Hendrickson. The Wild buzzed Colorado goaltender Patrick Roy with nine shots and had several quality chances in the third period, but couldn't score the equalizer. It was a thrilling final session of the year, with an inspired Wild team *pushing the President's Cup-winning Avalanche to the limit. Hendrickson, Walz and Gaborik all finished the season with a team-best 18 goals.*

Following the game, there was a dramatic farewell between the team and the thousands of fans in the building. Despite the loss, there was a celebratory atmosphere and the crowd gave a long, warm standing ovation to their Wild bunch. The players saluted the fans in return, giving away pucks, sticks, the jerseys off their backs and even the goal nets in a marvelous touch. And ever so slowly, the curtain fell on the inaugural season of the Minnesota Wild.

It was time for the playoffs, the games leading to the Stanley Cup finals and then the Cup itself, hockey's Holy Grail, the capture of which is every team's dream but the achievement of only one team each year. The Wild, having finished their season, would have to carry that dream to another time. But two teams were still playing in late spring. For the New Jersey Devils and the Colorado Avalanche, the dream was still alive.

Anaheim Scout Mike McGraw was sizing up the 2001 Stanley Cup finals, and he felt it was clear that both teams had the nice mix of players that all NHL clubs hope to assemble. "Each team has a blend of the highly skilled type of hockey player to go with the guys who are tough as rocks," said McGraw. "Sometimes a few of those guys are one and the same, which is how you end up in the Stanley Cup finals."

New Jersey has a guy who has busted his butt to stay in hockey, Brian Rafalski, who is about 5' 9" when he's got the right shoes on. He played at the University of Wisconsin and is a great player for the Devils, no matter what his size. When the Wild played New Jersey at home in mid-January, Rafalski didn't have one of his better games of the season, although the Devils won 4-2. "I didn't contribute that much tonight," said the little dynamo of a defenseman, who ended up with 52 points in the regular season and a phenomenal 18 points in the playoffs (better playoff numbers than Alexander Mogilny, Scott Gomez or Jason Arnott). "Give them credit, though. I don't know if I put a shot on net." He didn't that night. He took three shots, none of which was on goal. But he did have an assist on Alexander Mogilny's game winner late in the second period. It was one of his 43 assists on the year.

New Jersey is solid and can cover any one player's off night. They're so balanced that if one gun doesn't get you, the other one will. They generate reactions like Jacques Lemaire's answer the first time the Wild were preparing to play New Jersey, at the Xcel

Energy Center, when Jaques was asked if he was looking forward to playing his old team.

"Why would I be looking forward to playing them? I'm hoping they get lost and can't find their way over here; maybe they miss the plane or get caught in a snow-storm." He said it with a big grin, but it was clear he knows the New Jersey organization, he knows a lot of the players (having worked with Bobby Holik, Martin Brodeur and Scott Stevens, among others) and he recognizes what they are capable of accomplishing. He doesn't fear any team, he simply has respect for them.

Nevertheless, McGraw explained that he gave the edge to the Colorado Avalanche, based largely on the potential for overwhelming, series-defining play by the Avs greatest stars, Joe Sakic and Patrick Roy.

"Colorado has a couple guys who can win the Cup by themselves. Patrick Roy can win the Cup with the way he can shut a team down. Joe Sakic can get going on offense and win it with a spectacular performance. Those guys are that good. I also like the way Ray Bourque and Rob Blake (a late-season acquisition from the L.A. Kings) have covered for each other on the defensive end. I think Blake gives support to Bourque, and allows Ray to do a little bit more on offense."

The Avalanche also had an incentive to win a Stanley Cup for 20-year veteran Bourque, a popular and intense competitor who had not won a Cup during his many years with the Boston Bruins, or with Colorado in 2000. A lot of people around the Colorado franchise were hoping to see Ray get his name on the trophy.

One thing you recognize about both the Avalanche and the Devils is that the great teams are loaded with players just below the superstar level, who are a shade better than merely good, and who consistently get the job done. "It's all about having the proper components in the machine; getting the right nut to go with the right bolt," says McGraw. "Not having to rig the thing with washers, so to speak, to get the right fit. Both Colorado and New Jersey are teams that don't need to hide anybody. That is where the Wild are trying to go, and it's a process that takes time. Of course, Jacques Lemaire has done it before and that gives him an edge."

Darby Hendrickson has tremendous respect for the Colorado Avalanche and the talent of one Chris Drury, a sparkplug center on the Avalanche team, and a player who was especially tough on the Wild during the 2000-01 season. Hendrickson has played with Drury at the World Championships and regards him as "a superstar. He's a guy who can really play and capitalizes on opportunities as well as any player I know." Hendrickson also played with Chris's older brother Ted on the '94 Olympic Team, and has stayed with the Drury family out in Connecticut. "Those guys are a class act all the way," added Hendrickson.

To the winners go the spoils; Chris Drury scored 24 goals and garnered 41 assists in just 71 games during the regular season, had 11 goals (second only to Joe Sakic's 13) during the Stanley Cup playoffs and is a Cup champion with the Colorado Avalanche in 2001.

There's a pretty good chance that the Stanley Cup may have to make a detour to a favorite saloon on Washington Avenue in Minneapolis when Drury's teammate Shjon Podein, the Rochester native who played his college hockey at the University of Minnesota, Duluth, takes his turn with the prize. Podein, who had played for Edmonton and Philadelphia before coming to the Avalanche, is known as a tough practice player who pushes hard day in and day out, and one NHL scout spoke of a "tireless work ethic" that has served Shjon well.

Podein spoke positively of the Wild when he was in town for the January 12 Avalanche-Wild game, won 5-0 by the Avalanche. The game was closer than the score indicated, as Podein implied in saying, "They've been hot, and you can see why. They work hard every night, they don't give up much and they try to take care of their chances."

About 100 family and friends were expected to make the 75-mile drive from Rochester to see Podein play that night, and he said it would be the first time some of those folks had seen him play since he was in high school. "I'm excited, of course," he said. "The whole thing just feels so right." The big left wing, who used to watch North Star games from the cheap seats at the Met Center, paused for a moment and looked around the visitors' locker room at the Xcel Energy Center.

"Man, it's good to see NHL hockey back in Minnesota. Are you kidding? It's great to have hockey back here. It never should have left."

Both Hendrickson and Podein are guys who have had to battle to reach some stability in their hockey careers. Both have spent time in the minor leagues (the AHL) after breaking into the NHL. They have worked hard to get back to the top and have achieved success at the highest level of the game. Anaheim scout McGraw has respect for the battle native Minnesotan Brian Bonin and others have waged to escape from the minor leagues. "It's a hard fight to make it to the NHL for a number of good hockey players, with the clock usually working against them," said McGraw. "The AHL, it might be said, is a league where the thinking needs to be 'It's time to get moving if we're going to make it.' You've got to be tough to get out of the minors, physically and mentally."

That's why you have to admire a guy like Brian Bonin, who never gave up on playing at the highest level while toiling in the minor leagues. He did his job, worked hard and hoped for an opportunity, which finally came at the end of the Wild's first season. He was able to participate in some wonderful moments with the team, including the final celebration after the Colorado game. He's a tough guy and a very good hockey player, but it wasn't meant to be with the Wild. Bonin struggled to meet the demands Jacques Lemaire places on his forwards, and if the NHL is going to happen for Brian Bonin, it's going to happen somewhere else. At last report, he was playing in Switzerland.

Doug Risebrough wants to use the minor leagues as the prime training ground for future Wild players. He's not interested in developing the habit of dealing for guys to build his team, and has learned through experience that there are inherent risks in making trades. He believes some players will flourish in a new environment, and the Wild have plenty of guys who are doing just that. But as far as acquiring new players through trades to enhance the future, Risebrough is often leery. Maybe a player can do some good, maybe he will simply stagger along, or worse, perhaps he will disrupt the chemistry of a tight hockey club.

"When you are trying to find professional hockey players through trades, there is a lot to consider," said Risebrough. "It might seem a little unfair to say that players made available for a trade are damaged goods, but rarely will a team give up a 'jewel' without really working with him to the end. There may be a circumstance you can understand in which a guy was not successful, and you try to create something different for him in a new environment. We have done that with a few players, but I'm aware that you may be taking on a challenge when you make trades."

Risebrough anticipates that he will be able to keep, for the long term, the players he views as critical to the Wild's future success. He has a direct style that tends to work best when all parties involved are fully informed. He likes to be able to talk to players directly when need be, and he doesn't like agents who try to keep their clients off limits.

"I have no problem talking to players or agents," says Risebrough. "I believe the players have to accept responsibility for their own lives, and they should be able to handle my commentary or my criticisms. I've already had some discussions with players regarding how I see them fitting in, and I have no problem holding those conversations with an agent. I will say to the agent, 'I'm telling you this, and I want to have the ability to talk to the player and say the same thing.' That way, there's no confusion."

An East Coast hockey executive noted that Risebrough has had a chance to focus on which of his guys are the "jewels" and who could be expendable. "Those players on the Minnesota Wild during the first year of the franchise were given a great opportunity, a full chance to succeed or to fail on the ice. Jacques didn't leave a lot of questions for Doug Risebrough; Doug knows how these guys play, he saw them play in a lot of games and he saw the players for what they are. They were exposed, both good and bad."

That NHL insider believes certain tests are yet to come for the new franchise, and wonders if the two men will stay on the same page regarding ice time for the young players. Frequently, he says, there is a sense of urgency about developing them. "Will Doug tell Jacques at some point, 'The kids have to get more ice time, they need to play?' That happens with most new teams in due course. It's certainly possible, given the unique relationship between the two men, it won't happen like that. More "suggestions" than statements may be made by Risebrough regarding giving prospects a better look in the NHL, but only time will tell. I saw a lot of games this year, and they've convinced me this is a pretty unique situation."

SEVENTEEN

A BRIGHT FUTURE

There was a feeling at year's end, both in management and among the coaching staff, that the players from the inaugural season deserved a chance to succeed in the coming campaign. Doug Risebrough, for one, did not foresee big changes just for the sake of change. "I've said right along that these guys have earned an opportunity to help us move forward. I don't anticipate a lot of wholesale changes, and I think we have guys who will get better. They're going to have to.

"I really like our guys, but the players all know that performance is what drives it for us. We need to 'inch up' daily, as an organization and as a team; we have to keep finding ways to get better. We're going to need to improve and continue to grow every day. That's not just the first couple of years, that's going to be the first four or five years."

So it comes to an end, a grand and glorious season of hockey and of more than hockey. It's time to move on, for the players and the fans and journalists as well. The Minnesota Twins would play their baseball home-opener at the Hubert H. Humphrey Metrodome in Minneapolis after the season-ending Colorado Avalanche game. It's baseball season, not playoff time for the Wild. Defenseman Willie Mitchell will spend part of the off-season salmon fishing with his father and friends. The former New Jersey Devil is looking forward to it, and he speaks to me excitedly about the Vancouver fishing scene as he moves around collecting gear. The scar from the nasty seven-stitch cut he took in his first game with Minnesota is almost healed, and despite that blow he remembers the game positively; it was after that March 6 game with St. Louis that he turned to a group of reporters and said, "I can see this team never gives up. I said to Brad Bombardir right after the game, 'Hey, this is a good team.'"

He looks happy and is smiling a lot as he packs his bags. He earned some stripes this year, a big defenseman who proved himself adept at reading plays and playing a Jacques Lemaire style of defense. Willie was one of the best on the team at using his stick to disrupt traffic in the passing lanes and wasn't afraid to play the body of his opponent when necessary. "I don't have a rocket shot like Al MacInnis or skate 100 miles per hour like Scott Niedermayer or make monster hits like Scott Stevens, but I do everything pretty well."

He chalked up a big goal against Vancouver and had seven assists for eight points in just 17 games for the Wild and is hoping to make a bigger contribution in 2001-02. "This has been a great place to be," he adds. "I knew that this was a good place as soon as I got here, and everything looks good for the future. A great building and great fans, what more could you ask for as a player?"

Manny Fernandez and Sylvain Blouin are heading down to Mexico to do some fishing of a different kind, hoping to soak up the sun and enjoy the social scene. Sylvain finished the season in strong fashion, and appeared to grow in confidence as the season progressed. Hanging around with Manny, who never seems to lack for confidence and flashes a winner's attitude, has probably helped Sylvy, who finished with three goals on the season and a whopping 27 penalty minutes in *one game* on the road, at Nashville, the last day of March. These good buddies, the smooth goalie and the big left wing, never seemed to be too far apart off the ice, and had a lot of fun on it.

Manny's ankle injury at the end of the year was disappointing, however, and it still seems to nag him as he shuffles around the emptying locker room. "It's been a full year. I'm a little frustrated with the way it ended," says Manny, referring to his season-ending injury and the lack of team victories at the end of the campaign. Manny finished the year with a 19-17-4 record while playing in 42 games and set an NHL expansion record for lowest goals-against average, a solid 2.24 with a .920 save percentage.

I glance around the emptying locker room, which is missing most of the usual tools of hockey war, and think to myself; that's okay boys, enjoy the summer break. The 2001-02 battles will be here soon enough. We're going to need all of you fresh and healthy, ready to rock and roll in year two of the franchise.

Darby Hendrickson will head up north to break his Lund boat free of its shackles and catch some walleye, maybe play a little golf. But first, he's going to play in the World Cup for team USA. He will go on to star for the Americans, and score the overtime game winner in a stunning 4-3 victory over Canada in the semifinals. Darby will be leaving for Germany shortly after cleaning out his Wild locker. "You accumulate a lot of stuff over the course of the season," he tells me a bit sheepishly as he packs some bags following the season-ending Colorado game.

Hendrickson loves fishing and everything that goes with it. He loves being out on the water with his friends, his hockey buddies (and there are a few of them in northern Minnesota) as well as going fishing with wife Dana and the rest of his family, including new son Mason. He loves the singular feeling that exists in northern Minnesota when the walleye are biting. Fishing with light tackle and nailing the elusive walleye is what the good life is about for Darby. "Yeah, I love it," says Hendrickson, shortly after the first season is in the books. "We'll be heading up there real soon, and I can't wait to get out on the water. It's a big part of the reward for living up north."

Asked about his love of fishing, Hendrickson becomes thoughtful. "I like the fact that so many variables come into play, things like the structure of the lake bottom, the temperature of the water, the wind," he said, pondering the subject of his second favorite sport. "I really love the challenge. There's nothing like the feeling of knowing that you've found the fish after working hard for them. I like trying to make the most of the opportunity when you're on 'em."

On the water or on the ice, Darby Hendrickson is all about trying to make the most of his opportunities. The contract he signed during the summer of 2001 should keep him with the Wild for the next three years, and he couldn't be happier about it. "It's a good contract, and I'm glad to get that part of the business out of the way," Hendrickson said. "Let's play hockey!" he added with a grin.

The Minnesota Wild captured the "Let's play hockey" attitude sought by the Wild organization. Hendrickson, like other members of the team, seems genuinely appreciative of the opportunity to make a great living at

Darby Hendrickson relaxes at the lake.

what he loves to do most. The business stuff is incidental to the cause of playing high-caliber NHL hockey, and this team knows it.

"We all know this is a business as well as a sport, but we had such a good mix on this team for the first year, a strong chemistry that all teams try to achieve, and I want to focus on making our team even more successful," Hendrickson says. "No superstars, just a strong desire to build a strong team and play hockey. At the beginning of the season we didn't know how it was going to turn out, but I'm very satisfied with what we accomplished. We became a very tight team, and that's what chemistry is all about, becoming a stronger unit.

"The joy of this year was all about getting better," Hendrickson continues. "That was the most fun thing for all of us, I think, seeing how much we improved. We believed we could win any game. When you believe something like that, it's contagious! There was a tremendous feeling of "team" that we developed over the course of the year. I've really enjoyed going to the locker room every day and working with the people we have, a superior bunch of guys."

They became a stronger unit than anyone could have expected. The Wild took the season series from Chicago, Calgary, Tampa Bay and expansion partner Columbus. They took three of four from NHL "original-six" member Chicago and won their only game with Boston. The Wild notched several splits with teams in the league, including the Detroit Red Wings and natural rival Dallas, taking the first two games from the Stars.

So what teams might develop as rivals for the Minnesota Wild? Dallas, for sure. There's not much doubt that the intensity level regarding a Dallas game will remain high for both players and fans, probably for years to come. There was a lot of fire surrounding the Detroit games as well as, interestingly, Brian Burke's Vancouver club. Chicago may shape up as a strong rival, with proximity being a plus, certainly, and there's always something about the Chicago Blackhawks. There was a tradition of tough hockey games with the North Stars and it should be the same for the Wild.

Blackhawks owner Bill Wirtz was not a supporter of the idea of returning hockey to Minnesota, and for a period of time was in fact something of a roadblock. There is also the fact that the Wild kicked the Hawks around pretty good for a first-year team. After dropping the first game to Chicago at home, Minnesota dumped the Blackhawks three consecutive times, including twice on the road. Even the sleepy Chicago franchise should respond to that bullying by the newcomer.

You accumulate a lot of memories over the course of a long hockey season. One of the good ones at the end is of Colorado's Joe Sakic, moving quietly down the corridor after the Avalanche's season-ending victory over the Wild. Joe is on his way to get started with the business of winning his second Stanley Cup, but he pauses to tell an inquiring journalist that he likes the Wild's potential. "These guys could be trouble in a little while. It's a nice program they've got here," the mild-mannered Sakic says. "This building has a first-class feel and they're well coached. That lends itself to good results. They've played pretty tough hockey against us."

Nice words, I thought, from a fellow whose team went 5-0 against the Minnesota Wild, outscoring them 19-6 in the process. Colorado gave the Minnesota Wild a good look at the kind of mature, successful team they would like to be in years to come. The Wild are built more on the New Jersey model, with both the defensive scheme and a cost-conscious management reminiscent of Lou Lamierello's Devils, but who doesn't like the flourish with which Colorado plays?

The Wild need to get better to challenge the powers-that-be in the NHL, and they are going to take the incremental steps needed to improve the team for year two of the franchise. Sergei Krivokrasov and Jeff Nielsen are expected to move on, with the decision not to make a qualifying contract offer to Nielsen, "one of the toughest decisions we had to make," according to Doug Risebrough. "There has to be change, there has to be growth to get better." Krivokrasov may be offered the opportunity to return under different contract terms.

Nielsen had some real sparkplug games for the Wild, but he suffered a shoulder injury that cost him a lot of time. That probably made him more vulnerable to the process of change. That, and a bit of a numbers game with new players coming on board, according to Jacques Lemaire. Jeff played big against the Dallas Stars, helping the team get out of the gate fast with the first goal of that historic game. And against the Detroit Red Wings a couple of weeks later, he scored the fastest goal in club history just 0:26 into the game in the thrilling 3-2 Minnesota Wild overtime victory.

Expectations will be high for newcomers like Andrew Brunette, a scorer with good hands who had 59 points in 77 games for the Atlanta Thrashers in 2000-01, and Jason Marshall, a "tough, solid, 'defensive' defenseman," according to Tommy

Thompson. Marshall began the season with Anaheim and finished with Washington; Mighty Duck scout Mike McGraw also thinks highly of Marshall. "He's a great everyday player who takes his lumps and keeps pitching in," says McGraw. "He can dish it out, too. He should help the Wild."

Former Gopher and Anaheim Mighty Duck defenseman Mike Crowley became a part of the Wild organization, and coach Mike Ramsey thinks the Minnesotan's ability to bring the puck up the ice could be a plus. Thompson views Crowley as "a potentially strong contributor," though he will be battling a plethora of defensive players who are of good quality, among them Brad Brown, who has played with the Rangers, Hawks and Canadiens the past three years, and Travis Roche, who signed with the Wild and played the same day against Colorado in the team's final game. Nick Schultz has probably played enough junior hockey with Prince Albert of the Western Hockey League. *Worth remembering:* "The guys who were with us last year have an advantage as far as understanding the system," says Ramsey. "That may give them an edge."

Brunette and the "Latvian Lightning," Sergei Zholtok (big numbers with Montreal a couple years ago) are a couple of the players who have the potential to elevate things on the offensive end, maintaining the competition that is essential to growth as a team. It's the same thing with the goaltenders; Dwayne Roloson (who's had lots of NHL experience and an exceptional year in the AHL) and the solid (but young) Derek Gustafson look to contend for spots on the big league roster.

A Final Reflection

After watching a few more of the guys prepare to depart for the summer, it's time to take one last look at the sheet of ice that had been the scene of great victories as well as humbling defeats (and a few gut-wrenching ties), but certainly plenty of great moments. Some arena staff were moving around cleaning after the Colorado game, but in large part things are very still as I gaze out at the marvelous hockey palace. Taking a moment to reflect while perched on the Wild bench, sitting quietly amid the paper cup debris, the abandoned tape and the discarded Advil, there is a feeling of finality. All is properly silent. The inaugural campaign of the Minnesota Wild is finished.

Working my way out the big Kellogg Street doors of the Xcel Energy Center, I feel proud of how the new NHL team and its players acquitted themselves over the course of the year. The closing 4-2 loss to the Avalanche had been a typically solid hockey game, tight until the empty-net goal finished things up for the home squad.

Heading for my car parked on the street near the St. Paul Hotel (good tip: folks arriving early for a Wild game can sometimes snag a meter spot downtown), I feel the warmth of the sun's rays on my face. It has been a slow-starting, very wet spring up to this point, and it was a crummy, drizzly day when I arrived at the Xcel Energy Center in the morning. But I put the umbrella away as I walk in bright sunshine toward the hotel, feeling the gentle transition from winter to spring is finally in the air. I walk slowly, enjoying the stroll to the car on what is now a beautiful day.

Arriving at my parking spot, I wave to the doorman standing in front of the grand old hotel. The same hotel where Jac Sperling had made his home for over a year and a half while working to make the Minnesota Wild a reality, and where the press-dodging Jacques Lemaire had been registered under a female name while considering the Wild coaching position.

"Did they win?" yells the top-hatted gentleman, looking for all the world like a Dickensian character come alive in downtown St. Paul.

"No," I answer. "Not today. But they'll be back."

Because that's how it feels. The National Hockey League is back in town, and while the Minnesota Wild lost a few battles over the course of their inaugural season, they had won a number of wars, stretching well before the initial dropping of the puck. There was the building of a grand and glorious new hockey arena. The launching of a fine major league hockey and business organization. The demolition of the previous NHL hockey franchise, which had lit out of the Twin Cities seven years earlier. That demolition came both on the ice and, with the 6-0 drubbing of the Dallas Stars, in the minds and hearts of the new Minnesota Wild hockey fans. And they had witnessed the growth of a young hockey team, coming together and well-focused on a bright future.

One of these days soon, a large victory over a Cup-contending team like Dallas (defeated twice), Detroit (defeated twice) or Pittsburgh won't bring the euphoric rush it generated in 2000-2001. It will be workmanlike, a job accomplished and well done. It will be satisfying in a different and more complete way, perhaps. There will be a realization that the Wild have arrived, and it will be grand. There will be a more mature sense of joy.

Until then we will savor the new memories...

Wild fans witnessed the birth of a wonderful new tradition for hockey fans of all ages in the state of Minnesota, the State of Hockey. The 2000-2001 season was a tremendous ride for a first year team, with nothing but more fun and excitement planned for the future. It was victory with a capital "V" for the hockey fans of the Twin Cities, and I sensed great appreciation for the Wild organization's achievement. The grand vision had been realized, and it had truly exceeded the dream.

"When we started on this whole thing back in the mid–1990's, we thought we could do something special by restoring hockey to its rightful place in Minnesota, but there was no way we could have imagined how great it would turn out to be," Mayor Norm Coleman had said. "There was so much pure fun, that was had by so many people! The Minnesota Wild and the return of hockey have surpassed our expectations in many, many ways."

As I drive down Kellogg Boulevard, past the Xcel Energy Center on my way out of St. Paul, I want one last look at Minnesota's new hockey Mecca, where thousands of hockey fans had spent much of the winter. Sure enough, there's Bob Naegele, Jr., a key leader of this hockey expedition, out on the front steps talking with a small group of fans. He is animated as he speaks, gesturing and moving his head from side to side. As I slow to get a better look, I can see that Naegele is smiling that winner's grin of his. It was a heck of a sight to see, the visionary Wild chairman sharing his final moments of the season with the fans. It's a fitting close to a wonderful year of memories that are now a part of Minnesota hockey history.

MINNESOTA WILD
2000-2001 CLOSING NIGHT ROSTER

NO	PLAYER	POS	HT	WT	SHOOTS	B'DATE	BIRTHPLACE	1999-00 TEAM
2	Willie Mitchell	D	6-3	205	L	04/23/77	Port McNeill, B.C.	Albany (AHL)
3	Ladislav Benysek	D	6-2	190	L	03/24/75	Olomouc, Czech. Rep.	Sparta Praha
5	Brad Bombardir (A)	D	6-1	205	L	05/05/72	Powell River, B.C.	New Jersey
6	Travis Roche	D	6-1	190	R	06/17/78	Whitecourt, Alb.	North Dakota (WCHA)
10	Marian Gaborik	LW	6-1	183	L	02/14/82	Trencin, Slovakia	Dukla Trencin
11	Pascal Dupuis	LW	6-0	196	L	04/07/79	Laval, Que.	Shawinigan (QMJHL)
12	Matt Johnson	LW	6-5	235	L	11/23/75	Welland, Ont.	Atlanta
14	Darby Hendrickson (C)	C	6-1	195	L	08/28/72	Richfield, MN	Vancouver
16	Roman Simicek	C	6-1	190	L	11/04/71	Ostrava, Czech Rep.	HPK Finland
17	Filip Kuba (A)	D	6-3	205	L	12/29/76	Ostrava, Czech Rep.	Florida
19	Jeff Nielsen	RW	6-0	200	R	09/20/71	Grand Rapids, MN	Anaheim
21	Cam Stewart	LW	5-11	196	R	09/18/71	Kitchener, Ont.	Florida
22	Stacy Roest	C	5-9	185	R	03/15/74	Lethbridge, Alb.	Detroit
23	Pavel Patera	C	6-1	181	L	09/06/71	Kladno, Czech Rep.	Dallas
24	Antti Laaksonen	LW	6-0	180	L	10/03/73	Tammela, Finland	Boston
25	Sergei Krivokrasov	RW	5-11	185	L	05/15/74	Angarsk, C.I.S.	NSH/CGY
28	Mike Matteucci	D	6-2	210	L	12/27/71	Trail, B.C.	Long Beach (IHL)
32	Brian Bonin	C	5-10	186	L	11/28/73	Saint Paul, MN	Syracuse (AHL)
34	Jim Dowd	C	6-1	190	R	12/25/68	Brick, NJ	Edmonton
36	Sylvain Blouin	LW	6-2	207	L	05/21/74	Montreal, Que.	Worcester (AHL)
37	Wes Walz	C	5-10	180	R	05/15/70	Calgary, Alb.	Lugano
42	Andy Sutton	D	6-6	245	L	03/10/75	Kingston, Ont.	San Jose
44	Aaron Gavey	C	6-2	200	L	02/22/74	Sudbury, Ont.	Dallas
77	Lubomir Sekeras	D	6-0	183	L	11/18/68	Trencin, Slovakia	Ocelari Trinec

NO	GOALTENDERS	POS	HT	WT	CATCH	B'DATE	BIRTHPLACE	1999-00 TEAM
29	Jamie McLennan	G	6-0	190	L	06/30/71	Edmonton, Alb.	St. Louis
30	Derek Gustafson	G	5-11	210	L	06/21/79	Gresham, ORE.	St. Lawrence (ECAC)
35	Manny Fernandez	G	6-0	180	L	08/27/74	Etobicoke, Ont.	Dallas